The Integration of
Expert Systems into
Mainstream Software

CHAPMAN AND HALL COMPUTING SERIES

Computer Operating Systems
For micros, minis and mainframes
2nd edition
David Barron

The Pick Operating System
Malcolm Bull

Programming in FORTRAN
3rd edition
V. J. Calderbank

Expert Systems
Principles and case studies
2nd edition
Edited by Richard Forsyth

Machine Learning
Principles and techniques
Edited by Richard Forsyth

Expert Systems
Knowledge, uncertainty and decision
Ian Graham and Peter Llewelyn Jones

Artificial Intelligence and Human Learning
Intelligent computer-aided instruction
Edited by John Self

Artificial Intelligence
Principles and applications
edited by Masoud Yazdani
ACCESS
The Pick enquiry language
Malcolm Bull

Applicative High Order Programming
The Standard ML perspective
S. Sokolowski

The Integration of Expert Systems into Mainstream Software

Alan C. Gillies
Lecturer in Information Technology
University of Salford

CHAPMAN & HALL COMPUTING
London · New York · Tokyo · Melbourne · Madras

UK	Chapman & Hall, 2–6 Boundary Row, London SE1 8HN
USA	Van Nostrand Reinhold, 115 5th Avenue, New York NY10003
JAPAN	Chapman & Hall Japan, Thomson Publishing Japan, Hirakawacho Nemoto Building, 7F, 1-7-11 Hirakawa-cho, Chiyoda-ku, Tokyo 102
AUSTRALIA	Chapman & Hall Australia, Thomas Nelson Australia, 102 Dodds Street, South Melbourne, Victoria 3205
INDIA	Chapman & Hall India, R. Seshadri, 32 Second Main Road, CIT East, Madras 600 035

First edition 1991

© 1991 Alan C. Gillies

Printed in Great Britain by T.J.Press (Padstow) Ltd, Padstow, Cornwall

ISBN 0 412 39930 X   0 442 31358 6 (USA)

British Library Cataloguing in Publication Data

Gillies, A. C.
  The integration of expert systems into mainstream software.
  I. Title
  006.3

  ISBN 0-412-39930-X

Library of Congress Cataloging-in-Publication Data

Available

To my wife, Jenny

Contents

Acknowledgements

Many people have contributed to this book. My colleagues at the IT Institute in Salford have been very helpful. In particular, Lorraine Baric, Phil Baugh, Paul Bowker and John Rae have provided direct input for the book. Other research colleagues have been instrumental in shaping many of the ideas presented herein, particularly Anna Hart. My wife, Jenny, and my friend, David Walker, have ensured that what reached my publishers was at least intelligible. The publishers have been very helpful in getting this book to press, and my editor, Ellen Taylor, who inherited the project at a late stage, has been particularly efficient. I remain, however, responsible for the contents and all abusive comments should be directed to me.

Overhead projector slides and questions for tutorial discussion to accompany this book are available from the Departmental Administrator, Information Technology Institute, University of Salford, Salford, M5 4WT, UK.

Preface

The idea for this book grew out of the ES'88 conference held in Brighton in December of that year. The conference, held under the auspices of the British Computing Society's specialist group in expert systems, had taken as one of its themes 'integration'. I felt at the time that the conference was sadly lacking in papers supporting this theme. The book has taken a couple of years to come to fruition, during which a number of factors have influenced its development. The first major change came when I moved to the Information Technology Institute at Salford University, which provided a much broader IT environment within which the ideas could develop. The second change has been a gradual recognition by both industry and academics that integration of expert systems could be beneficial, and a growth in the number of tools available to support integrated system development.

The book is aimed at a practically-minded audience. The first major audience is in industry, either system developers and software engineers who are seeking to take advantage of expert systems, or expert systems developers seeking to turn their neat ideas into commercially acceptable products. The second major audience is the academic audience. The book is designed to include enough material to enable its use as a teaching text upon Bbc and MSc courses. However, it makes no pretence of being a 'standard' text on expert systems, and its use is envisaged on courses where expert systems are taught as part of a broader view of IT. This includes the Bbc and MSc courses at Salford, and BIT degrees at other institutions. It may also be used to teach expert systems in a way that is accessible to students with a strong software engineering background, as part of more traditional computer science courses.

The chapters can be grouped as follows: Chapters 1 to 3 introduce the basics of expert systems and what is meant by integration in this book. Chapter 1 looks at the basic questions, 'What is an expert system?', and 'What is integration?'. Chapter 2 introduces the basic concepts and terms of expert systems. Chapter 3 looks at the case for integrating expert systems with other software disciplines and outlines some principles for integration. Chapters 4 to 6 examine in greater detail the implications of integration under three principal subject headings. Chapter 4 looks at the software engineering consequences in the light of current methodologies and tools, concluding with an outline framework for integrated system development. Chapter 5 looks at the implications for human/computer interaction, developing a three-way model of interaction appropriate for integrated expert systems and examining in some detail, the vital question of allocating tasks within an integrated solution. Chapter 6 looks at quality issues, starting from current quality models and examining their effectiveness for all types of system. Some ideas are presented for a framework for the measurement of quality able to cope with the problems of expert systems. Chapters 7 to 9 present three case-studies: examples of successful integrated solutions from three very different applications. Chapter 7 is based upon a research project to provide automatic fringe pattern analysis with limited optical and computing hardware. Chapter 8 describes an American military decision aid, which provides a very different view of integration. Chapter 9 looks at an expert database system designed to provide advice upon taxation problems. Chapters 10 and 11 form a conclusion to the book. Chapter 10 is designed to show how the lessons learnt from the book and particularly the case-studies may be used to tackle the readers' own problems. Chapter 11 sums up where we have reached in the development of integrated systems and where the future may lead us.

The book is not designed to promote a particular point of view, but rather to stimulate the reader into their own thoughts and ideas. If it achieves this objective, then it has succeeded. It is also intended to be enjoyable, so if you enjoy reading it, so much the better!

Alan Gillies
Salford, 1990

Trademarks

The following trademarks are referenced within the text:

Ada	Department of Defense, Ada Joint Program Office.
C + +	AT&T Bell Laboratories, Inc.
DEC	Digital Equipment Corporation
Excelerator	Index Technology Corporation
GEM	Digital Research, Inc.
IEF	Texas Instruments, Inc.
Ingres	Ingres Corporation
Macintosh	Apple Computer Inc.
MS-DOS	Microscoft Corporation.
Sun View	Sun Microsystems, Inc.
Sun Tools	Sun Microsystems, Inc.
Turbo Pascal	Borland International, Inc.
Turbo C	Borland International, Inc.
Turbo Prolog	Borland International, Inc.
UNIX	AT&T Bell Laboratories, Inc.
Windows	Microscoft Corporation

Introduction: expert systems

'Artificial intelligence' (AI) has been sought after for a long time. The ancient Greek philosophers speculated on the possibilities long before computers were thought of. In this century, the computer has seemed to offer the first realistic means of achieving this goal. Early work was directed at producing general problem-solving programs and this ambitious goal was not attained. The next attempts to produce 'intelligent' systems were confined to narrow, specific problem domains. The results became known as 'expert' systems, and their success is still a matter of debate. It may be argued that a third generation of systems, known as knowledge-based systems (KBS), have met with greater success by taking still less ambitious goals. Partly because of their historical roots in AI research, these 'intelligent' systems have developed separately from other information systems . This is a source of pride to some researchers, but a major stumbling block to the acceptance of such systems by IT practitioners.

1.1 What is an expert system?

At the start of a book, it is generally useful to define our terms. In a book on expert systems, it is particularly useful to define the term 'expert system'. So here goes ...

'An expert system is a piece of software that seeks to model the expertise of a human expert within a specific problem domain.'

As you read the book, you will form your own opinion of the effectiveness of this definition in describing the breadth of systems that exist under this banner. This definition is offered as a starting point for our study, not the finish. Expert systems are part of the wider field of study known as 'artificial intelligence' (AI) and this is, perhaps, where the problems begin. AI is the field of subjects concerned with making computers behave intelligently. It includes areas such as robotics, pattern recognition and artificial neural networks as well as expert systems (Fig. 1.1).

The area of AI had been a subject for debate long before computers were available. Philosophers such as Descartes argued over whether people could be thought of as machines. With the advent of computers, the debate focused on whether computers could be made to think. An early attempt at an 'intelligent' program was made by Newell, Shaw and Simon (1957–1967). The aim of the work was to produce a general problem solver (GPS). The generality of the GPS meant it was inefficient and superficial in its analysis. The initial hope was for an artificial all-purpose system that would 'think' in a generalized way like the GPS of Newell *et al.*

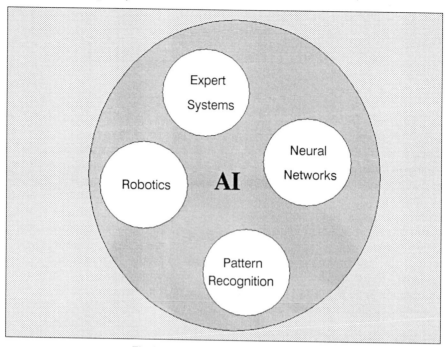

Fig. 1.1 Some of the disciplines within AI.

The lesson from early systems such as the GPS has been the realization that the successful encapsulation of knowledge is most easily attained within a specific and narrow problem domain. This has led to the concept of expert systems as systems which model expertise within a narrow and specific domain. Within such domains, some notable successes have been achieved, e.g. XCON (McDermott, 1985), the DEC computer configuration system. It is noticeable, however, that the same case-studies are constantly quoted. The favourite examples are still MYCIN (Shortliffe, 1976), a medical diagnosis system, PROSPECTOR (Duda and Reboh, 1984), a geological advice system and XCON (*ibid*), the computer configuration system previously mentioned. Of these, only XCON has enjoyed significant commercial use. There are two possible explanations for this. The first is that successful systems are being kept secret for reasons of commercial and military confidentiality, and this is undoubtedly a contributory factor. However, the second explanation is that the number of successful systems is still relatively limited, and this is likely to be true as well.

Today, there is still a mystique surrounding the subject of AI, and consequent confusion about what can be achieved in practice. So let's start by trying to clear up some misunderstandings:

Computers do not think for themselves. An artificial intelligence program is a program like any other. It is a set of procedures which the computer follows, with inputs and outputs.

AI programs use a symbolic representation of the world. All computer programs are based upon a model of the problem they seek to solve. In conventional information systems, this model is constructed in terms of numbers. In an AI program, the model is constructed in terms nearer to a human view using symbols, such as text or pictures. The computer's view is still a model, but is simply expressed in different terms.

Machine intelligence is not human intelligence. Human intelligence is a very broad and varied thing. Some of the characteristics of intelligent behaviour are reasoning, deduction, learning and adaptability. Machine intelligence seeks to model this behaviour, but is only able to do so in limited domains and in limited areas. Many machine intelligence techniques focus on one or two aspects of human intelligence, often at the expense of others, e.g. the so-called artificial neural networks have a greater ability to learn than expert systems, but do not provide justifications for their outcomes.

These points are summarized in Fig.1.2. With these constraints in mind, you may wonder why people bother with artificial intelligence at all. The answer is that computer systems offer a number of potential advantages, including speed, consistency, accessibility to expertise, the ability to handle complexity and cost. In the commercial arena, it is the latter which usually provides the driving force.

Expert systems are perhaps the most common form of AI system. The label 'expert system' is not applied to one single type of system, or to even a class of systems but to a whole spectrum of systems. It covers systems ranging from conventional information systems with hardly any symbolic reasoning content, to systems which depend entirely upon symbolic reasoning, and bear little resemblance to conventional information systems. Similarly, it is applied to systems ranging from those which use a very superficial symbolic model of a problem, the so-called 'toy' domains, to those which use very sophisticated symbolic models.

The use of the term 'expert system' for such a wide range of systems has been addressed by Modesitt (1987), who attempts to classify systems according to the level of their performance:

'Expert Systems are computer-based software systems which attain or surpass human expertise, currently in very narrow and specialized domains.'

Using this definition, he suggests that in 1987 there were only 60 to 120 such systems in use around the world, most internally by large corporations. He contrasts expert systems with knowledge-based systems (KBS), which he states

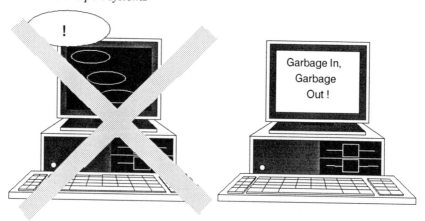

Computers do not think

In formation systems use a numerical model of the world. People use a symbolic view, with words and symbols.

Machine intelligence is not the same as human intelligence

Fig. 1.2 Machine intelligence.

involve knowledge of less depth and sophistication than that employed by human 'experts':

'KBSs are much less pretentious in their claims of expertise. They do embody heuristic knowledge (rule-of-thumb, best guess etc.) captured from intelligent sources. However they are a superset of expert systems, and thus should not claim expert-level performance.'

A similar distinction has been made by Ostberg (1988), who divides systems into two groups, high level and low level, according to the complexity of the system's analysis of the problem.

The problem associated with such analyses is that it encourages a value judgement according to the cleverness of the symbolic reasoning within the system. The more complex the analysis of the problem, the more complex the resulting system will be. Associated with greater complexity are greater problems in terms of establishing traditional software values of reliability, efficiency and maintainability. This is indicated by Modesitt's 1987 estimate of a small number of working systems that fitted into his expert system category. Other authors, such as Buchanan (1986) put the figure even lower. Optimists will point out that several years have now passed, but little hard evidence of rapid growth in this sector has appeared outside of the laboratory. In this book, the term expert system will be used in its broadest sense, because the philosophy behind integration suggests that the value of a system is based not upon how clever it is, i.e. its depth of symbolic reasoning, but rather upon its value to the user as a solution to a problem.

It is part of the hypothesis behind this book that mainstream expert system development has gone down a particular avenue. This avenue is characterized by systems designed as stand-alone systems, with an emphasis upon maximizing the depth of symbolic reasoning. These two characteristics both have problems associated with them.

The concentration on 'stand-alone' expert systems has inhibited the cross-fertilization of ideas from conventional software and the use of graphics and other software disciplines in conjunction with expert systems. A classic exception to this is the case of DENDRAL (Lindsay, 1980), an expert system for the analysis of mass spectroscopy data, which utilizes algorithms alongside rule-based heuristics. In spite of the success of DENDRAL, it has done little to inspire a similar approach to other problems.

The emphasis upon maximizing the depth of symbolic reasoning reflects the research background of many systems. The requirements of a research prototype system are different from a working commercial system. There is a need to promote traditional good software practice amongst expert systems to produce systems that are reliable, maintainable and efficient. These properties are often in direct conflict with flexibility and depth of symbolic reasoning. This conflict between flexibility of systems arising from greater depth of symbolic reasoning, and the traditional software virtues is illustrated in Fig. 1.3. As the depth of

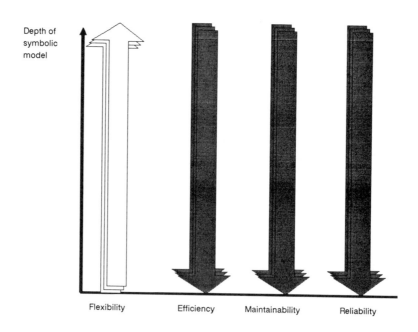

Fig. 1.3 Quality criteria as a function of depth.

symbolic reasoning increases, the task of providing reliable, maintainable and high quality software becomes more difficult.

This is borne out by the number of laboratory AI systems that never reach the commercial environment. If the aim is a practical working system, it is desirable to use the minimum depth of reasoning required to solve the problem in hand, in order to maximize the chances of achieving a high quality solution. In a research environment, this approach can appear unexciting and lacking in innovation. There is a need to bridge this gap in objectives if expert systems are to reach their commercial potential. There is also a great challenge to researchers in developing better systems which provide both depth of reasoning and traditional software virtues.

1.2 Are expert systems different?

The expert system community remains part of the AI community, and as such guards its exclusivity jealously. The case has been made by a number of authors that expert systems are fundamentally different from other information systems e.g Waterman (1986). He argues that expert systems have four characteristics that distinguish them from conventional software:

Expertise ; depth ; symbolic processing ; self-knowledge.

Consider each characteristic in turn:

(a) Expertise. In specifying expertise, Waterman states that expert systems must perform well, that is, at a comparable level to human experts and at a comparable speed. Even within a limited domain, this is a tall order for any computer system. Whilst systems may match performance in one area such as speed, it is unlikely that a system can match a human expert across a whole range of performance parameters such as reliability, error monitoring and adaptability. Most systems are developed because of the lack of access to, or excessive cost of human expertise. They do not set out to supercede their source human expert.

(b) Depth. AI scientists distinguish real world problem domains from so-called 'toy' domains. A toy domain is characterized by gross over-simplification, and by results that are consequently of little use. Thus an expert system that avoids such over-simplifications is considered to have depth. In a practical context, the required depth of a solution is dependent upon the problem. An efficient solution will make use of sufficient depth to solve the problem. The pursuance of depth *per se* is detrimental to the effectiveness of the solution, and so many effective solutions do not meet the desired criteria of depth.

(c) Symbolic processing. This refers to the use of symbols to represent objects rather than numbers. Symbols are manipulated by expert systems, whereas conventional information systems manipulate numbers and solve numerical equations. In a pragmatic solution, the system designer will make use of non-symbolic reasoning where appropriate, because of its advantages in reliability and efficiency.

(d) Self-knowledge. An expert system has knowledge about itself, enabling it to reason about itself. This enables it to provide a form of explanation of its actions. The ability of the system to impart knowledge about itself is potentially a great boon. However, failure to consider user issues at the earliest possible stages of project development can lead to both ineffective provision of 'explanation' and provision of a working system that does not address the correct problem.

This set of characteristics undoubtedly describes a type of system distinct from conventional systems. The problem is that the set of characteristics is so discriminating that it's hard to find a working system that fits this description, 'expert' or otherwise.

The systems that have been developed and are proving to be commercially advantageous fail to meet such purist requirements in a number of ways. The purist approach to 'expert systems' has not been helpful to the adoption of such techniques by software engineers, since it has led to systems lacking in traditional software virtues, and a certain amount of prejudice on the part of both expert system designers and software engineers. We may place alongside Waterman's idealized characteristics, a number of features which have also sadly been associated with many 'expert systems': inefficiency, unreliability, a poor user interface and major maintenance problems. Where this has occurred, part of the reason has been a wilful determination not to learn lessons from mainstream software.

The view of the author is that expert systems should be viewed as a particular type of information system, and as such should be considered alongside other distinctive types of system such as database management (DBMS) systems or executive information systems (EIS), shown in Fig. 1.4.

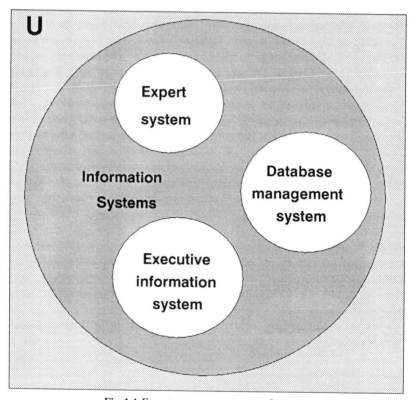

Fig. 1.4 Expert systems as one type of system.

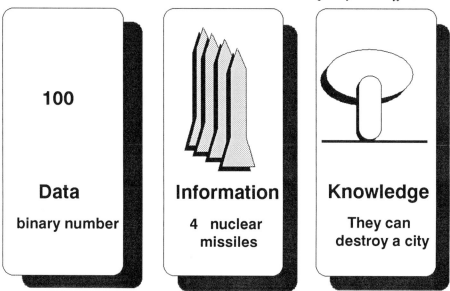

Fig. 1.5 Data, information and knowledge.

They should be required to conform to the same standards of performance and quality as any other system. Expert systems are distinct in terms of their approach to problem representation. Information systems process information, expert systems attempt to process knowledge.

In order to understand why expert systems are different and hopefully useful, we must establish what we mean by 'information' and 'knowledge'.

We may consider three types of representation on computers: data, information and knowledge. Data is the bare representation in binary numerical terms. Information is the same data, but with associated meaning. Because of that meaning, the information has value. Knowledge adds context to that information, providing greater meaning and, therefore, greater value. It is this greater value which feeds the self-importance of many designers of expert systems.

Consider the example shown in Fig. 1.5. As a piece of data the binary number 100 (decimal 4) does not convey much. The information 'four missiles' adds significant meaning to the data. The knowledge that four missiles could destroy a city is more significant still and forms the basis for making tactical decisions in a defence scenario. There is a similar progression in processing (Fig 1.6).

However, the representation of knowledge on a computer is limited by the fact that ultimately we must reduce that knowledge to data. This means in practice that we can only represent a subset of human knowledge on a computer. This subset of human knowledge is less rich than human knowledge and, therefore, might well be considered as information in a human context.

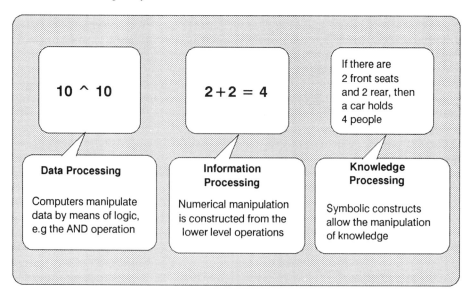

Fig.1.6 Data, information and knowledge processing.

Consider the following example.

In an expert system designed to assess the suitability of a person for a job vacancy, the personality characteristics of the candidate must be matched to the requirements of the job. We may assess the candidate's personality in terms of a number of types e.g dominant-aggresive, submissive-pleasant, assertive. In order to elicit which type of person we have, we may ask them a series of questions, such as

'Do you relish competition in your job?',
'Do you regard your presentations as energetic and dynamic?'
'Do you hate to fail?'
'Do you regard offense as the best form of defence?'

A dominant-aggressive person might be represented as a decisive person who likes competition, is energetic and dynamic and is absorbed with their own progress. Therefore, we would expect them to answer the questions positively.

Faced with such a series of question, many people will be dissatisfied by the requirement to answer 'Yes' or 'no' to questions requiring greater subtlety. They may also resent the crude labelling of people as simply dominant or aggressive. People cannot be summarized in such a simple way. This reflects a lack of depth in the computer-represented knowledge about the person, which is in fact made up what we would regard as a series of pieces of information, such as 'decisive', or 'competitive', in a human context.

The description of a person in such a shallow way is what workers in the AI field call a toy description. It would be dismissed as unrepresentative of 'true' AI. Unfortunately, the real world is made up not of 'toy' representations and 'real' representations, but of a continuous spectrum.

The depth of computer represented knowledge will always fall short of the subtlety of human knowledge because even if it were theoretically possible to represent human knowledge completely, it would not be feasible to store the data required. Consider the analogy of a sine wave, and a digitized representation, shown in Fig 1.7. At a slow sampling rate, the digitized form is a poor representation. This represents a toy domain. At the faster sampling rate, we have a better representation. At some point, we will achieve an adequate representation, but only at infinitely fast sampling will we achieve a perfect model of the sine wave in our digital form. If we seek to solve problems, the key to a successful solution is providing a model of sufficient accuracy or depth for our purposes. This is true whether our model is represented in numerical or symbolic terms.

The distinction between the use of symbols and the use of numbers lies at the heart of the distinction made between knowledge and information in a computing context. Humans use symbols to convey information. For example, the equation

$$2 + 2 = 4$$

makes use of symbols to convey both numbers and the addition operation. In computing terms this is a numerical and, therefore, information-based approach. Similarly, a description of a person as 176 cm tall, weighing 55 kgs may be regarded as numerical, or information-based in computing terms. The description of the same person as competitive, dynamic and decisive is symbolic and, therefore, in computer terms, knowledge-based.

In the solution of a problem, it is likely that the most effective model will involve both numerical and symbolic representations. This will require integrated rather than stand-alone expert systems. In the next section, we will consider how integration may be achieved.

1.3 Current trends towards integration

The historical exclusivity of expert systems has been challenged as a result of a number of factors:

(a) The apparent success of expert systems in the laboratory, judged by the literature, has not been matched by their uptake in industry.
(b) When judged by conventional software quality criteria, expert systems have often been found to be lacking in the traditional virtues of reliability, maintainability and efficiency.

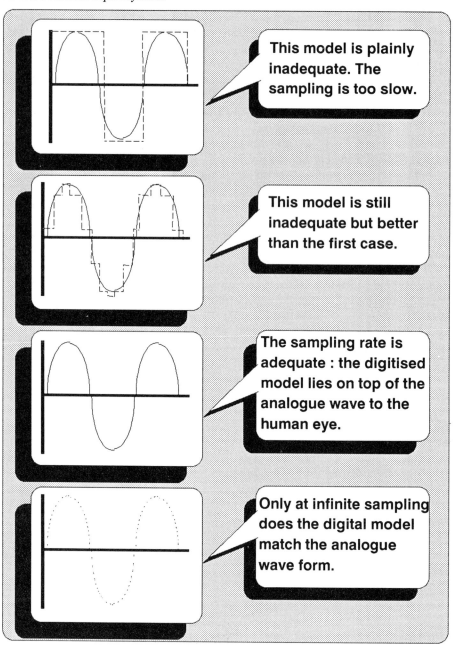

Fig. 1.7 Sine wave sampling : analogy of depth.

(c) Where industry has adopted expert systems, they have been of the 'low-level' type, tackling simple problems, making extensive use of numerical computation, and lacking in the features normally associated with a 'high-road' expert system.

A typical system of this type would be a simple diagnostic tool, built using an expert system shell representing knowledge which could also be represented in a chart or set of tables. Very limited explanation is provided. Its chief merit is its speed of operation, and increased reliability over its manual counterpart. The system runs on the PC on a manager's desk, and despite a lack of expertise, depth and self-knowledge, it will probably be embraced with enthusiasm, because of its low development cost and accessibility.

In such cases, the distinction between conventional and expert systems is distinctly blurred. Many of them utilize only limited symbolic reasoning, which could be implemented more efficiently and reliably in a third generation language (3GL), such as C or Pascal. This is not intended as an indictment of such systems. Any system which provides useful and cost-effective results for the user, should not be criticized lightly. The accessibility and convenience of such systems has been a beneficial process in terms of bringing expert systems out from the AI closet, but it has reinforced the prejudice of many software engineers that expert systems are toys, not 'real' systems.

Consider an analogy from the sphere of high fidelity audio reproduction. The introduction of compact disc players into mass-market audio systems, manufactured by consumer electronics companies, has brought fulfillment and music into many homes. However, it has also reinforced the view amongst many die-hard enthusiasts that compact disc is only suitable for dabblers and not for real enthusiasts, who remain loyal to their LP records.

In truth, the existence of accessible, low-level systems neither prejudices or enhances the potential of expert systems in larger software projects. The potential for a system which has both the traditional virtues of expert systems and the reliability and efficiency of other information systems is an attractive one. Work has started in a number of areas, for example, integration of expert systems with database management systems (DBMS) and with CAD and graphics.

The aim of this book is to show how the conventional software engineer can make use of expert systems technology, without throwing away all that has ever been learnt about software engineering. This may be achieved at three different, but complementary levels, illustrated in Fig 1.8.

(a) *The concept level.* Concepts from mainstream software can be incorporated into expert systems or vice versa. For example, user modelling could be incorporated into expert systems, increased use can be made of symbolic reasoning in conventional software through constructs such as 'IF..THEN..ELSE'. This has the advantage that system designers do not need

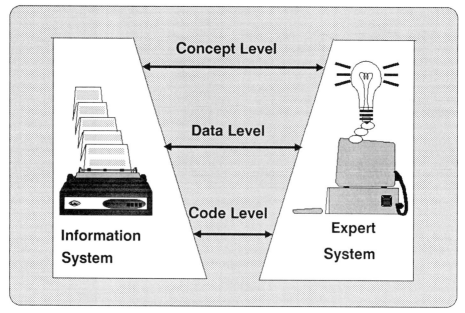

Fig. 1.8 Three levels of integration.

to leave the comparative security of their own camp. At the same time, its impact is likely to be limited.

(b) The data level. Interfaces have been implemented to allow data interaction, notably between expert systems and DBMSs. This allows separate development of each system, and is less limited than integration at the concept level, but such a system is faced by a tradeoff. The closer the links between the system, the better the system integrity, but the harder independent system design becomes.

(c) The code level. Integration at the code level requires a structured modular approach to program design. Individual modules can then be designed along knowledge-based and information-based principles.

As we move from integration at the concept level through the data level to the coding level, we bring greater advantages in terms of flexibility, integrity, efficiency. However, we face greater problems as well. Tools and methodologies have been devised for distinct information systems and expert systems, rather than integrated solutions. 'Add-on' systems e.g. adding an expert system to interrogate an existing database become more difficult to implement as interdependency increases. This book is principally concerned with integration at the code level, but along the way, we will see how integration at the two shallower levels has been achieved.

1.4 Further reading

A good general introduction to the subject of expert systems :
Waterman, D. (1986) *A Guide To Expert Systems,* Addison-Wesley.

These research papers describe two of the early classic expert systems: MYCIN and PROSPECTOR respectively :
Shortliffe, E.H. (1976) *Computer-Based Medical Consultations: MYCIN* , American Elsevier.
Duda, R.O. and Reboh, R. (1984) AI and decision making: the PROSPECTOR experience, in *Artificial Intelligence in Business*, (ed.) W. Reitmann , Ablex Publishing Corp., New Jersey,111–147.

CHAPTER TWO

Expert systems and their limitations

Expert systems have often been victims of their own hype. Competent performance, where it occurs, has been frequently disguised by a failure to fulfill unrealistic claims made by their designers. It is the purpose of this book to examine such claims and to provide a guide to potential pitfalls for the unwary. Like any information system, expert systems have a safe range of operating conditions, outside of which the results produced will be unreliable. Because of their special characteristics, they show particular problems in construction and use, which should be borne in mind.

In this chapter, the components and construction of expert systems are considered, with a particular emphasis upon some of the limitations, in order that the reader may gain a view of the safe operating limits of expert systems. The limitations of 'shells' will be discussed, and the processes of knowledge acquisition and representation are examined.

2.1 The knowledge representation problem

The first and arguably most difficult stage in the design of any information system is defining the problem, and then gaining sufficient understanding of it to produce a system. There is a 'knowledge gap' between the client and the system designer. The client knows about the problem, but does not know about computers. The system designer knows about computers, but not about the problem (Fig. 2.1).

Fig. 2.1 The knowledge gap.

In software engineering, we define the specialist role of analyst, to elicit the client's requirements and translate them into a specification for the implementation programmer to work from.

In expert systems, this role is taken by the knowledge engineer. If the role of the analyst in appeasing all parties appears difficult, the job of the knowledge engineer can appear nigh on impossible.

The job of capturing the knowledge to be used in the system is usually referred to as the 'knowledge acquisition' stage. It is generally considered to be a bottleneck. Where knowledge elicitation may be carried out successfully, there remains the problem of representing knowledge upon a computer. These two processes are closely linked, since the mechanism for knowledge representation will influence the knowledge acquisition process.

2.1.1 Knowledge acquisition

The process of knowledge acquisition has been well covered in Hart (1989). The principal method adopted for knowledge acquisition is interviewing a person with expertise in the problem domain. This process may be considered in three phases: pre-interview, main interview, post-interview, as shown in Fig. 2.2.

(a) *The pre-interview.* This consists of a preliminary knowledge gathering exercise, reading books and articles to gather a basic knowledge of the subject. It will be necessary to glean a basic vocabulary, so that the knowledge engineer can communicate effectively with the domain expert.

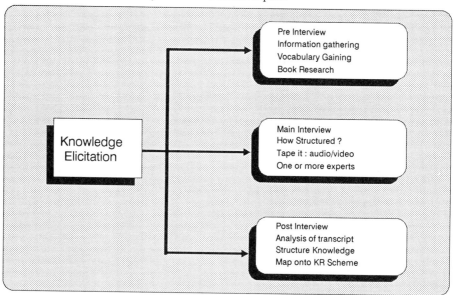

Fig. 2.2 The interviewing process.

(b) *The main interview* is usually tape-recorded. Audio taping is generally used, but video may be useful if graphical information is required, or the expert makes extensive use of gestures. The form of the interview may be structured, semi-structured or exploratory. In a structured interview, a questionnaire may be used to provide the structure. The danger with structuring is the risk of imposing inappropriate limits on the domain expert. At the other extreme, an exploratory interview may degenerate into a ramble.

(c) *The post-interview*. At the post-interview stage, the information must be organized into a form suitable for knowledge representation.

2.1.2 Knowledge representation

We shall consider three types of knowledge representation schemes in detail, rules, semantic networks and frames. In particular it must be borne in mind that the choice of scheme will strongly influence the process of integrating expert systems with conventional software.

(a) *Rules*. The commonest form of knowledge representation is in the form of rules. For example, the XCON expert system uses rules to represent knowledge concerning the configuration of VAX computers. An example of a rule from XCON is given in Tab. 2.1.

In rule-based representation, the expert's knowledge is represented by standard propositional logic, in the form of conditional statements:

XCON example rule

IF the current job is layout and assigning power supply

AND IF an SBI module has been put in a cabinet

AND IF the position it occupies in the cabinet is known

AND IF there is space in the cabinet for a power supply

AND IF there is an available power supply

THEN put the power supply in the cabinet in the available space.

Tab. 2.1 An example rule from DEC's XCON system.

IF predicate **THEN** consequent, e.g.
 IF the train runs late   *(predicate)*
AND IF I am in a hurry   *(predicate)*
THEN I wish I was in a car. *(consequent)*

A predicate is a condition which may be evaluated on the input of some information. The consequent is the result of one or predicates being evaluated in this way.

The rules in an expert system are manipulated by the inference engine. It may be of one of two types, forward or backward chaining. The two mechanisms are illustrated in Figs. 2.3. and 2.4. In backward chaining, the inference engine works by proceeding backwards from a hypothesis to those rules that have the hypothesis as the consequent. Consider the following example.

A professional society has four different classes of membership: full, associate, affiliate, student. Full membership is intended for practicing experienced professionals who have both academic qualifications in the field, and professional experience. It may be taken up by people in four categories:

- Those with a degree in the subject and at least three years experience.
- Those with the society's Part II examinations and at least three years experience.
- Those with a degree in a related subject and at least six years experience.
- Non-graduates with at least 10 years experience.

For those with less experience, associate membership is offered. The entry requirements are either,

- a degree in the subject but less than 3 years experience, or
- part II examinations but less than 3 years experience, or
- a related degree or Part I examinations plus 3 years experience, or
- more than 5 years experience.

Those new to the profession are offered affiliate membership, and student membership is available for those students aspiring to the profession.

As the method adopted is backward chaining, we work back from the possible outcomes through the decisions required to reach those outcomes. The possible outcomes in this case are the four classes of membership, full, associate, affiliate, student. The decisions leading to those classes have been arbitrarily labelled 1-6. The criteria for the different types of membership are organized into a decision tree in Fig. 2.5.

The six questions required to elicit the information are:

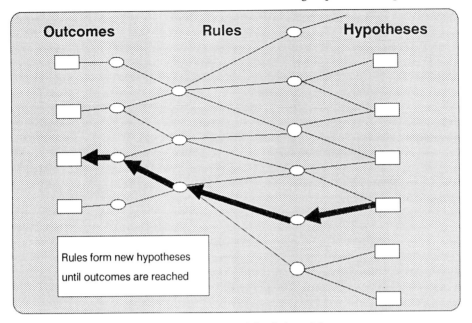

Fig. 2.3 Backward chaining (schematic).

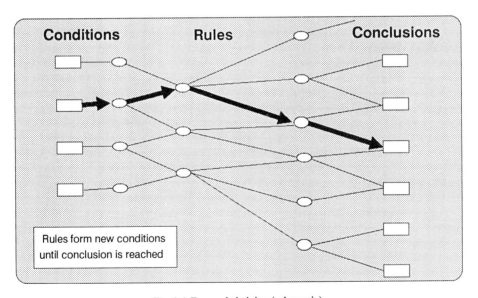

Fig. 2.4 Forward chaining (schematic).

```
PROGRAM Membership :
TYPE
String : ARRAY [1..80] OF char :

VAR
DegreeInSubject, DegreeInRelatedSubject : boolean ;
PartIexamination, PartIIexamination, student : boolean ;
Yearsexperience : integer ;
response : char ;

BEGIN
DegreeInSubject : = false ;
DegreeInRelatedSubject : = false ;
PartIIexamination : = false :
PartIexamination : = false ;
Writeln ('Have you a degree in the subject ?' );
Readln (response);
IF  (response = 'y') OR (response = 'Y') THEN
DegreeInSubject : = true ELSE
BEGIN

Writeln ('Have you passed the part II professional exams ?' );
Readln (response);
IF  (response = 'y') OR (response = 'Y') THEN
PartIIexamination : = true
ELSE
BEGIN
Writeln ('Have you a degree in a related  subject ?' );
Readln (response);
IF  (response = 'y') OR (response = 'Y') THEN
DegreeInRelatedSubject : = true
END {Degree in related subject ?}
ELSE
;
```

Tab. 2.2 Pascal source for membership scheme.

```
BEGIN
Writeln ('Have you passed the part I professional exams ?' );
Readln (response);
IF (response = 'y') OR (response = 'Y') THEN
PartIexaminations : = true
ELSE
BEGIN
Writeln ('Are you a student' );
Readln (response);
IF (response = 'y') OR (response = 'Y') THEN
student : = true ;
END ; {student}
END ;{ Else part I examination }
END ;{ degree in related subject}
END ;{ Else part II examination }

Writeln ('How much experience do you have ?') ;
Readln (Yearsexperience);
IF (DegreeInSubject) OR (PartIIexaminations) THEN
CASE  Yearsexperience  OF
3..99 : Writeln ('You are eligible for full membership');
0..2  : Writeln ('You are eligible for associate membership') ;
END {CASE} ;
ELSE
IF (DegreeInRelatedSubject) OR (PartIexaminations) THEN
CASE  Yearsexperience  OF
6..99 : Writeln ('You are eligible for full membership');
3..5  : Writeln ('You are eligible for associate membership') ;
0..2  : Writeln ('You are eligible for affiliate membership') ;
END {CASE} ;
ELSE IF  (student ) THEN
Writeln ('You are eligible for  student membership')
ELSE CASE  Yearsexperience  OF
9..99 : Writeln ('You are eligible for full membership');
5..9  : Writeln ('You are eligible for associate membership') ;
0..4  : Writeln ('Sorry, You are currently ineligible for  membership');
END {CASE} ;
END.
```

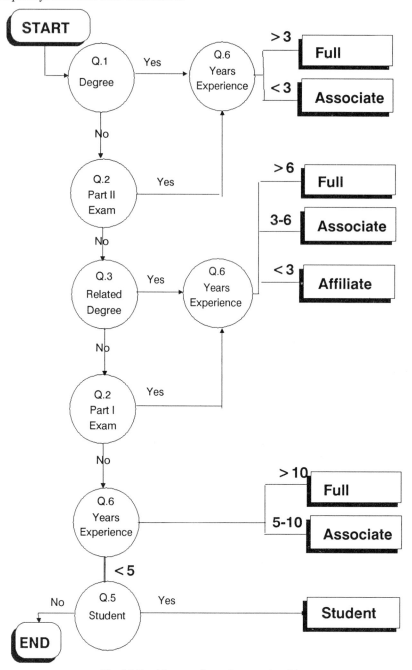

Fig. 2.5 Decision tree for society membership.

1. Have you a degree in the subject?
2. Have you Part II examinations?
3. Have you a degree in a related subject?
4. Have you Part I examinations?
5. Are you a student?
6. How much experience do you have?

A resulting implementation in Pascal is illustrated in Tab. 2.2.

In forward chaining, each rule is examined, and the truth of its predicate evaluated. The consequents of those predicates testing true are added to the knowledge base, and the process continues until the truth of no further consequents may be added. In this process, the reasoning from consequent of one rule to the predicate of another forms a forward chain.

The process of forward chaining may be represented in a number of steps:

Step 1. The system is presented with a condition or set of conditions.

Step 2. For each condition presented, the system searches the rules for those that correspond to the condition in the predicate, i.e. the IF part.

Step 3. Each rule can then generate new conditions from the invoked THEN part (consequent), by finding those rules where it occurs as predicate. These are added to the existing conditions.

Step 4. If there are any new conditions, the process returns to Step 2 and repeats until there are no new conditions.

Consider the following example.

The traditional characteristics of software quality include efficiency, structuredness, and maintainability. These are related to each other, and also to other factors, such as the level of language employed for implementation. The links between these different properties are summarized in a set of rules in Tab. 2.3.

IF SoftwareEfficiencyRises   THEN StructurednessFalls

IF SoftwareEfficiencyFalls   THEN StructurednessRises

IF 4GLemployed   THEN SoftwareEfficiencyFalls

IF AssemblerLanguageEmployed THEN SoftwareEfficiencyRises

IF StructurednessFalls   THEN MaintainabilityFalls

IF StructurednessRises   THEN MaintainabilityRises

Tab.2.3 Rules from the forward chaining example.

Now let's tell the system that we are going to implement our system in a fourth generation language (4GL), and see what conclusions the system arrives at.

Step 1. The condition is *'4GLemployed'*
Step 2. Finds one rule with corresponding predicates:
　IF 4GLemployed THEN EfficiencyFalls
Step 3. Matching for efficiency falls produces new condition:
　StructurednessRises
Step 4. Return to Step 2 with *StructurednessRises as condition.*
Step 2. Finds one rule with corresponding predicates:
　IF StructurednessRises THEN MaintainabilityRises
Step 3 No new conditions.
Step 4 STOP

The conclusions are those conditions found by the system in step 2:

　IF 4GL employed THEN
　1. Efficiency Falls
　2. Structuredness Rises
　3. Maintainability Rises

Forward chaining rapidly becomes very inefficient as system complexity increases, since each new fact added to the knowledge base requires a reassessment of the truth of each rule, and therefore, the overall computational cost rises dramatically with each initial condition.

Rule-based representations are very common. Apart from the general problem of achieving a meaningful representation of the required knowledge, they show a number of problems:

Computational Overload. Large rule sets quickly give rise to maintenance problems, unless structured into independent rule sets. This is a basic lesson from software engineering which is commonly accepted for expert systems. They are inefficient to run, and may even exceed physical memory constraints. This is a particular problem where a number of unusual examples are cited by experts . 'The exception that proves the rule' anecdote may cost as much as the rest of the system put together in terms of rules. The importance of handling such cases must be carefully considered.

Side Effects due to Multiple Evaluation. Rule predicates are generally assumed to be evaluated once. Where they are evaluated more than once, this can cause unwanted changes in the knowledge base, leading to spurious results.

Assigning Certainty Factors. It is generally insufficient to record an expert's judgement in terms of true or false. It is often necessary to assign a certainty value,

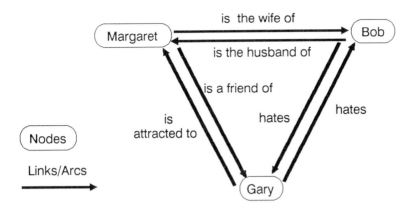

Fig. 2.6 Semantic network example.

usually between 0 and 1 to cover 'grey' cases. The problem of quantifying certainty values is large. The problems in maintaining consistency across a large system is immense!

(b) *Semantic networks*. A second approach is the use of semantic networks. A semantic network consists of a set of nodes, connected by links or arcs. A node describes an object (noun) or a descriptor (adjective). The links describe relationships such as 'is a' or 'has a'. A semantic network is illustrated in Fig. 2.6.

One attraction of this approach is the ease with which it maps onto AI languages such as PROLOG, by means of simple sentences. Consider the trivial example given, from which six sentences may be derived:

Margaret *is the wife of* Bob
Bob *is the husband of* Margaret
Margaret *is a friend of* Gary
Gary *is attracted to* Margaret
Gary *hates* Bob
Bob *hates* Gary

The six sentences may be represented in PROLOG using the construct action(Subject,Object):

is the wife of (Margaret,Bob)
is the husband of (Bob, Margaret)
likes (Margaret,Gary)
is attracted to (Gary,Margaret)
hates (Bob,Gary)
hates (Gary,Bob)

The knowledge base built up in this way may then be interrogated:

Railway Locomotive		
Propulsion	Electric	
		RESTRICTION (Value : Text)
		RESTRICTION (Content : one of Steam/ /Diesel/Electric)
		RESTRICTION (Number of values = 1)
Class	87	
		RESTRICTION (Value : numeric)
		RESTRICTION (Value Range 1..199)
		RESTRICTION (Number of values = 1)
Maximum Speed	140	
		RESTRICTION (Value : numeric)
		RESTRICTION (Value Range 1..150)
		RESTRICTION (Number of values = 1)
Operating Region	**West Coat Main Line from Euston to Manchester/Liverpool/Preston/Glasgow**	
Currently In Service	**True**	
		RESTRICTION (VALUE-TYPE logical)
		RESTRICTION (One of True/False)
		RESTRICTION (Number Of Values = 1)
Frame	**Slots**	**Values** **RESTRICTIONS**

Tab. 2.4 Example frame describing a locomotive.

e.g.?-likes (Margaret,Gary)   *yes*
?-hates (Bob,X)   *Gary.*

(c) *Frames.* The third type of knowledge representation scheme is the frame-based approach. The particular strength of this approach is its ability to structure knowledge. A frame is a structure for holding various pieces of interrelated knowledge. The frame is made of slots, in which the pieces of knowledge are stored.

Slots may contain a single value or a set of values. Values are not restricted to numerical values, but may be of many types e.g. symbolic, logical, graphical, text, numerical (integer, decimal or floating point). Restrictions may be placed upon values associated with a slot. Restrictions may be placed upon acceptable value types or upon the acceptable range of values or both. The frame is represented schematically in Tab. 2.4. The implementation of frame-based knowledge is discussed in the next section.

Frames are helpful when a structure is apparent in the expert's knowledge. By arranging frames in a hierarchical structure, with more general frames at the top of the hierarchy and more specific frames at the bottom, we may arrive at a knowledge base which is arranged in a similar way to that used in many reasoning applications. This allows for inheritance of properties down a hierarchy of frames. Inheritance of properties in frames may be compared to human inheritance. Consider the following family tree:

In our human family tree, we would expect some inheritance of common characteristics such as blue eyes, brown hair and so on. We might also expect

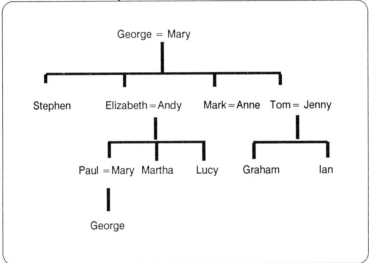

Fig. 2.7 Inheritance in people : a family tree.

transmission of genetic defects. For example, if George is colourblind then genetics tells us that his daughter Elizabeth will be a carrier of the defective gene, and that her son Paul can expect to be colour blind. As the gene is not transmitted by the male offspring, it will not appear in other branches of the family. However, should Paul have any female children at a later date, they will become carriers themselves. Human inheritance is a complex business due to rearrangement of the genetic material at fertilization.

Inheritance within frame-based reasoning is simpler because a 'child' frame is derived from a single parent and simply inherits all its properties. Thus a 'child' frame inherits all the properties of its parent frame

As an example, consider the hierarchy of locomotives shown in Fig. 2.8.
Since an electric locomotive is a subclass of locomotive, it will inherit the general properties of a locomotive. Since a Class 87 locomotive is a subclass of electric

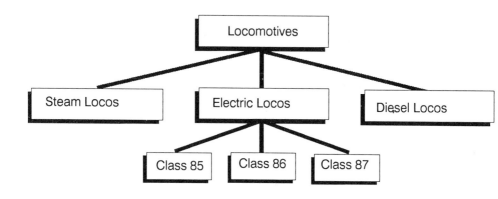

Fig. 2.8 Example hierarchy : railway locomotives.

locomotive it will inherit the general properties of electric locomotives. Inheritance may involve a value or simply a slot. Alternatively, inheritance may involve the restriction upon a value. Inheritance may simply be totally restricted in which case null inheritance occurs. Inheritance is useful where a change in a slot is made near to the top of a hierarchy, since by inheritance, the consequences of this change are made to all frames lower down the hierarchy.

Frames can bring a number of advantages to knowledge representation:

- Structuring the knowledge base
- Reducing the number of rules, thereby increasing clarity

- Reducing complexity for testing
- Increases traditional software virtues associated with structure e.g. maintainability and reliability.

The implementation of frame-based reasoning has generally been achieved through the use of object-oriented programming techniques using environments such as SmallTalk. Inevitably, therefore, implementations inherit the attributes of such environments. The principal drawback of such environments is their inefficiency. As in conventional software, there is a trade-off to be made between structuredness and efficiency. In some cases, the price in terms of lost efficiency may be prohibitive. However, recently a number of object-oriented dialects of conventional third generation languages such as C and Pascal have emerged, such as C+ +and Turbo Pascal, v.5.5. These include data structures which allow the manipulation of objects. The object data type may be compared to a record in standard Pascal. Implementation using object-oriented techniques is discussed below.

2.1.3 Knowledge mapping

The process of translating a domain expert's knowledge into an expert system may be viewed as a sequence of mappings (Fig. 2.9).

At each stage, the knowledge becomes more structured and defined. At the same time, at each stage, there is the risk of either mistranslating the knowledge or

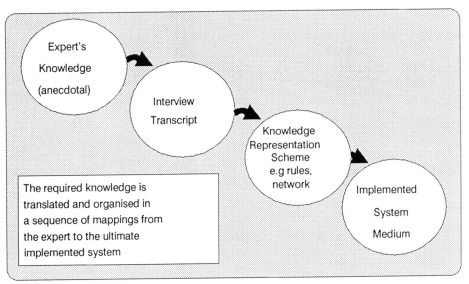

Fig. 2.9 Mapping knowledge from expert to system.

coming across a part of the knowledge that cannot be successfully mapped onto the next phase. At the interview stage, a number of problems may be encountered.

- Expert knowledge is generally anecdotal and a group of experts may produce conflicting anecdotes.
- The knowledge engineer has to make decisions based upon little knowledge of the domain.
- Experts may be resistant to the whole idea, feeling that their knowledge is devalued if it can be represented as a set of hard and fast rules (Fig. 2.10).

Fig. 2.10 Expert reaction may not be favourable.

At the end of the interview, the knowledge engineer is faced with translating the interview transcript into rules or some other knowledge representation scheme. Domain experts are often unable to help at this stage. They may not recognize their knowledge in this form, even if it produces the answer they expect. Many problems genuinely do not seem amenable to analysis in this way.

Some of the most successful systems are those where the problem is already presented in terms of rules. For example, the transportation of nuclear waste has been the subject of a successfully implemented expert system. This problem is governed by the safety regulations laid down by the Government. As such, the knowledge is inherently rule-based. Whilst the regulations themselves are not necessarily suitable for incorporation into a rule-based knowledge base, the basic expertise is amenable to this kind of rule-based analysis.

The mapping from a knowledge representation scheme to the implemented system is often more straightforward, since representation schemes have been designed with system implementation in mind. This reflects the fact that representation schemes are designed with the end system in mind rather than the problem. If the overall process is seen as bridging the gap between the form of knowledge in the expert's head and the knowledge represented in the system, then knowledge representation schemes are there to provide an intermediate stage. This intermediate stage, however, does not lie centrally between the expert's knowledge, but rather nearer to the system knowledge (Fig. 2.11).

As a consequence, the mapping of knowledge from expert to knowledge representation scheme is often described as a bottleneck in the overall process. The problem may in fact be insoluble, as many people believe that genuinely expert knowledge is far too subtle to be represented effectively by any computer model, whatever type of representation is employed.

2.2 Implementation media

Expert systems are computer programs and can be written in almost any computer language including standard third-generation languages such as Pascal or C. Systems have even been written in BASIC, but this has been done generally as an academic exercise to prove its feasibility than a serious attempt to build an implementable solution. Simple propositional logic may be implemented effectively in Pascal or C, but for more complex knowledge representation, specialist implementation techniques and languages are required.

Many languages, tools and environments have been developed to facilitate translation of knowledge in a machine-representable form into a working program.

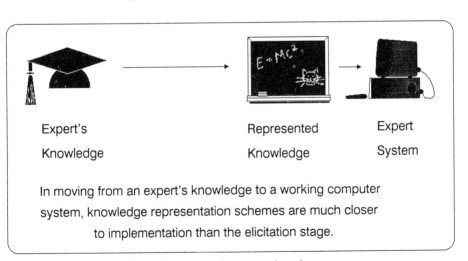

Expert's Knowledge   Represented Knowledge   Expert System

In moving from an expert's knowledge to a working computer system, knowledge representation schemes are much closer to implementation than the elicitation stage.

Fig. 2.11 The role of representation schemes.

Unfortunately, these have often contributed to the isolated position of expert systems within the software community.

Three approaches to implementation will be examined below: shells, PROLOG and object-oriented programming. Particular attention will be paid to how they match knowledge representation techniques and whether they allow for integration.

2.2.1 Expert system 'shells'

The most common implementation medium used in expert systems is the expert system 'shell', a tool to assist in the development of expert systems. In what appears to be an attempt to confuse the uninitiated, these tools are often simply referred to as 'expert systems', in much the same way that database management systems are sometimes simply called databases. A shell is not a system, it is an implementation tool or environment.

The popularity of these 'shells' has been attributed to a number of factors:

- They run on PCs under DOS.
- They are generally quick and easy to use.
- They eliminate the need for 3GL programmers.
- They are good for prototyping.
- They provide limited explanation facilities.

The principal reason for their success lies in their association with the PC. There are no hard and fast generalizations that can be made about usability. In spite of claims, the ease of use of such systems is highly variable. Experience of teaching students has shown that several shells use a syntax which is at least as involved as that of a 3GL. The attempt to free the system designer from the need to consult a programmer has been replaced by a dependence upon domain experts and knowledge engineers.

The consequence of the popularity of shells has been a perpetuation of the view of expert systems as stand-alone, PC-based, 'quick-and-dirty' systems. This has led to systems lacking many of the features that software engineers would look for in good software, such as maintainability, modularity, efficiency and usability. In seeking to widen the appeal of expert systems amongst software engineers, it is necessary to provide systems acceptable in terms of current software engineering practice.

To consider why shells are limited, let's go back to basics and start with the components of an expert system. An expert system may be considered in terms of three components (Fig. 2.12).

The knowledge base. The knowledge base contains the knowledge used by the system, being broadly analogous to the data in a conventional system. The

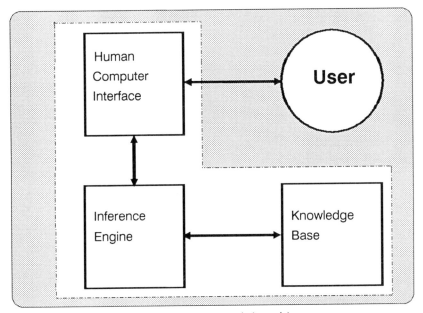

Fig. 2.12 Expert system (schematic).

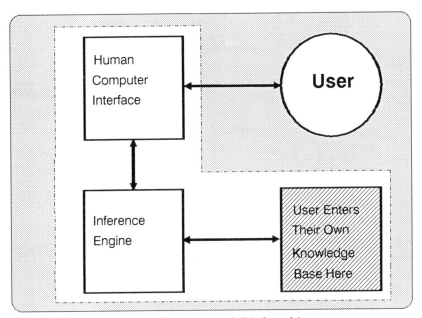

Fig. 2.13 Expert system shell (schematic).

knowledge may be stored in the form of rules, frames or some other knowledge representation scheme.

The inference engine. The inference engine manipulates the knowledge as a program manipulates data. The inference engine may be implemented in a number of media, a 3GL, an expert system shell, an AI language such as PROLOG or using object-oriented techniques.

The interface to the user. The human/computer interface allows the system to communicate with the outside world. In a system integrated at the data level, typically with a DBMS, there will also be an interface to other software systems.

The theoretical basis for expert system shells is that the knowledge base can be removed from an expert system, leaving a framework into which a system designer can slot their own knowledge base (Fig 2.13). The problem with such a view is that it is oversimplified. The knowledge base and inference engine are not wholly independent ; they are invariably linked. The knowledge base is a product of the knowledge representation scheme employed. The inference engine is influenced by the problem domain and its operation depends upon the choice of knowledge representation scheme. There is no such thing as an application-independent inference engine.

Perhaps the greatest problem associated with shells is really a human misapprehension. This is known as the scaling problem. The accessibility of shells means that they are used to produce small-scale systems quickly. The real problem starts after this. It has often been assumed that these small-scale systems may be readily expanded to produce larger scale systems. This is not the case. Complexity increases rapidly with system size, and it is this complexity which poses the biggest headache to the system designer. Complexity requires managing in the software development process, and shell-based development procedures do not encourage this.

The practical consequences are that shells are generally effective when used on small problems, where the application is similar to the one from which the shell was drawn. Thus, EMYCIN, the shell derived from the medical diagnosis system MYCIN has been applied to a number of diagnostic problems.

Shells have a number of limiting characteristics arising from these fundamental properties:

Limited in scale, versatility and complexity. The limits on the versatility and complexity provided by shell-based systems lead to their use for small-scale, rapid prototyping systems. They do not provide the basis for the more reliable, more complex systems associated with conventional software engineering. In this they share many of the attributes of fourth generation languages, although they are not as user-friendly or powerful as 4GLs in general.

Shells are inefficient. Many of the operations available in shells could be handled within a conventional 3GL. Where such comparison is possible, 3GLs are vastly more efficient in terms of runtimes. As a result of the limited versatility of many shells, it is arguable that the price of comparatively little extra flexibility is a great loss in efficiency. Although computing power is getting cheaper, many PCs are still comparatively limited in power, so that efficiency is still an issue in such systems.

The interface is limited. Shells are generally designed for simplicity, and are often designed with the PC in mind. As a consequence, the provision for human/computer interfaces is limited, although some of the newer shells do make some provision for interface design.

It should be mentioned that some shells are designed to run on machines such as VAX minicomputers. However, such systems lose the primary attraction of PC-based shells: accessibility. An experienced VAX user should have no worries in tackling a full-blown AI language such as PROLOG, or implementing in a 3GL such as C. The prevalent view of expert systems remains shell-based, PC-based and consequently, lacking in software engineering credibility in terms of handling complexity, and in a lack of traditional virtues such as maintainability, testability and reliability, to name but three.

Some of the newer shells, known as second-generation shells, have gone some way to addressing the worst limitations of earlier products. However, they are still generally tied to a vision of expert systems as stand-alone systems or with limited interaction with database systems. They do not facilitate the freedom of integration that is desirable if an optimum solution is to be achieved. So other options should be considered.

2.2.2 PROLOG

The third generation languages such as C and Pascal are known as procedural languages because they are expressed in terms of procedures and functions. Prolog, by contrast, is known as a declarative language which expresses a problem in terms of facts and rules, lending itself to the implementation of symbolic reasoning developed with an AI prototype.

PROLOG lends itself to implementation of a number of standard AI representations and this should be borne in mind at the design stage if PROLOG is to be used for the implementation. PROLOG may be used to represent rules and facts:

e.g.,
bigger_than (elephant, mouse)

This is a PROLOG fact which states that in English, 'An elephant is bigger than a mouse.

e.g.,
rich (person) if has (person, money)

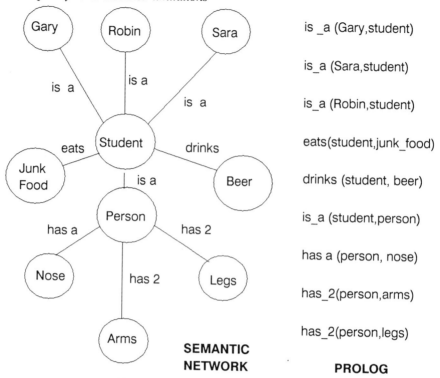

Fig. 2.14 Semantic network showing inheritance.

A rule which translated into English says, 'A person is rich if they have money'

We have already seen (Fig. 2.6) that one of the attractions of semantic networks is that they may be easily represented in PROLOG. Consider the more complex example shown in Fig. 2.14. This example illustrates how inheritance may be handled in PROLOG. A student is a person, so inherits their properties and Gary is a student, inheriting the properties of both students and people. Because of its ability to handle complex data types, and the relationships between them, including the inheritance of properties, PROLOG may also be used as an object-oriented language, described below. It is this flexibility that make PROLOG an attractive proposition. Further details of the language may be found in Clocksin and Mellish (1987).

However, in the past, PROLOG has suffered from a number of limitations which have limited its effectiveness and use. It has changed in character in recent years in a number of ways which make it more useful to practical problem-solvers and particularly to those seeking an integrated solution:

Wider acceptance. PROLOG was developed in Canada and Europe and therefore was at a disadvantage in the influential American market place. In recent years, it has been accepted and adopted by many US software developers. PC versions have become available which genuinely offer the facilities of larger compilers.

Compiler Efficiency. As recently as five years ago, many PROLOG compilers were prohibitively inefficient in terms of the code they produced. Modern PROLOG compilers are much more efficient, and more competitive with procedural languages.

Additional Features. PROLOG compilers have moved from the realm of the laboratory to the office PC and are aiming to compete in the same market as expert system shells. A number of 'popular' compilers such as Turbo Prolog have emerged which combine the features of PROLOG with the convenience traditionally associated with C or Pascal environments through such features as:

- Interface building tools.
- Comprehensive I/O facilities.
- Operating system interface.
- Floating point arithmetic.
- String handling.

Aids to Integration. Some PROLOG compilers offer a range of facilities which make them particularly attractive to the integrated system designer. In particular, many compilers now permit interfacing to a 3GL, usually C, allowing PROLOG modules to exist within a C program. Further, some offer an integration with a DBMS, either with an internal database, or by providing interfacing facilities to an external database.

2.2.3 Object-oriented programming

The origins of object-oriented programming (OOPS) lie in an attempt to place more emphasis within programming upon the data. The technique depends upon a model of the problem made up of 'objects'. An object is a specific example of a 'class'.

Thus in terms of traditional Pascal nomenclature, an object is like a variable, and a class is like a data type. The difference between an object, that is an instance of a class and a variable that is an instance of a type such as a Record, is that an object may have code associated with it as well as data. This is represented in the class declaration as procedures as well as data variables. This is illustrated by the example in Fig. 2.15.

The description of the property 'King's Cross station' as a record can only be made in terms of data. The object describes the processes associated with that property. Within the board game 'Monopoly', the property may be bought, resold or mortgaged.

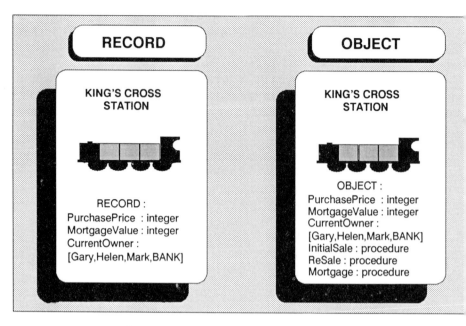

Fig. 2.15 Comparison of record and object structure.

```
TYPE

Electric = OBJECT

MaxSpeed : integer ;

MaxPower  : integer ;

PullTrain          :
procedure :

:

:
```

Tab. 2.5 OBJECT declaration in
extended Pascal.

```
TYPE

Electric = OBJECT |

OBJECT (locomotive)

MaxSpeed : integer ;

MaxPower: integer ;

PullTrain : procedure :

:
```

Tab. 2.6 Inheritance in extended Pascal.

OOPS was developed through dedicated environments such as SmallTalk, but for integrated systems, the most useful implementations are the object-oriented dialects of traditional 3GL languages such as Turbo Pascal, version 5.5 and C++. OOPS is particularly useful in the implementation of frame-based reasoning. The representation of inheritance will be considered as an example.

Turbo Pascal (v5.5) declares classes using the keyword OBJECT which is declared as a datatype in a similar way to a record (Tab. 2.5).

Inheritance is facilitated by the association of classes with a parent class at the time of declaration. Thus, from the hierarchy of locomotives the class locomotive may be declared as a parent of electric (Tab. 2.6). This language has been described in detail recently in a book by Shammas (1989).

A corresponding object-oriented dialect of C, C++, has become popular with C programmers. A detailed account of C++ has been given by Lippman (1989). In this case, the class is declared as 'Class'. From the same locomotive example, a class describing locomotives in C++ would be declared as

Class *Locomotive*

Electric is a subclass of locomotive, and electric locomotives inherit the general properties of locomotives. This would be represented in the form :

Class *Electric* : public *Locomotive*

Similarly, the type 87 electric locomotive is a subclass of electric locomotive :

Class *Type87* : public *Electric*

(The keyword public controls the access of the system to the class concerned)

Within the C++ language, the classes may be manipulated using a number of operators.

Within an integrated solution, if knowledge is represented in terms of frames and frame-based reasoning, then we may integrate the processing of such knowledge using classes and class derivation within C++. The information content also be implemented within C++, using the features of standard C. The small detailed differences between C and C++ are unlikely to pose major problems. C++ may be compiled in a similar way to standard C, and produces executable binary code. Similarly, Turbo Pascal v5.5. incorporates all the features of earlier implementations so integration occurs naturally at the source code level.

In later chapters, we shall see how successful integrated solutions have been implemented.

2.3 The special features of expert systems

It can be dangerous to take analogies too far between expert systems and other information systems. They have characteristics and problems all of their own. In particular, the way that different types of systems go wrong must be examined. Let's start by considering an information system. Take possibly the most famous computer anecdotal story of all time. A gas bill arrives on the doormat for £1000054.12p. After berating the rest of the family for excessive use of the gas-fire, the householder arrives at the showroom. Inevitably, the chorus is raised, 'Oh, it's the computer's fault'. On hearing this, the software engineer smiles indulgently, and gently reminds people that computers do not make mistakes: garbage in means garbage out, but a computer will always produce the correct answer arising from the data provided, assuming it is operated within its correct limits.

When we are dealing with information systems, there is a correct and verifiable answer. When we move to expert systems, we are dealing with subjective judgements: the human experts may not even agree. It is no longer possible to define a correct solution and, therefore, to say whether the computer is right or wrong. The twin problems facing the expert system designer are how to decide what is an error, and having decided upon some error criteria, how to find these errors.

In a typical problem tackled by an information system, the answer is right or wrong. Provided the computer is programmed correctly, it should produce a consistently correct answer. Problems to be tackled by expert systems are fuzzy in nature, and are unlikely to have a simple correct solution.

Take as an example the weather forecast. Whilst human meteorologists make extensive use of computers to collate and analyze data, the final analysis is carried out by a human using judgements. The forecast is expressed in symbolic terms e.g. warm, dry and sunny, as well as numeric terms 20°, 0.01 mm rainfall and 13 hours of sunshine. Although we constantly criticize forecasts for being wrong, it is generally fairer to assess their effectiveness as partially right.

In information systems, errors may arise at various stages of the software lifecycle. At the specification stage, errors may arise leading to a faulty specification. Even if the specification is correct, the designer may implement the system incorrectly, i.e. not in accordance with the specification. Where the system is implemented in accordance with the specification, errors may arise if unforeseen conditions lead to the computer exceeding its correct operating limits, e.g. integer overflows, array bounds errors.

Testing is designed to show where errors occur so that they may be eliminated. testing is generally carried out in two stages; unit testing at the implementation stage and acceptance testing which ensures that the system as a whole performs to its specification.

Expert systems face a number of additional problems. The specification of an expert system is generally revised during the project. Most expert systems development methodologies are of the prototyping school rather than the lifecycle school. (For those not familiar with the distinctions, these are explained in Chapter 4). It is often difficult, therefore, to test whether such systems are performing to their specification. Many expert systems are not developed as discrete units, therefore, it is also difficult to carry out effective unit testing.

Where testing is possible, errors may not be easy to spot. The knowledge engineer works with an imperfect knowledge of the domain. A conclusion cannot be judged as correct or incorrect, but rather only as adequate or inadequate.

Testing strategies for expert systems are often based upon comparing performance with human experts . This is fraught with problems. The reference human judgements are rarely 100% reliable, and the experts themselves may disagree. Ask two opposing politicians for an economic strategy, and then ask yourself how you can measure their performance. Now imagine setting up two computers each with an expert system aiming to encapsulate the knowledge of the politicians, with the increased uncertainties associated with knowledge transfer from human expert to machine, and try to establish the criteria for judging the success or failure of each system.

In practice, the expert system can only be tested by examining all the possible outcomes and checking that they fall within the bounds of adequacy defined for the system. Leaving aside the problem of defining the criteria of adequacy, we are left with the problem of testing all possible outcomes. The stereotype of expert systems as small shell-based systems has obscured this problem. A true expert system with expert level performance is by definition complex, since expertise is complex. Small systems that do not attempt expert level performance can be thoroughly tested if the number of possible outcomes is small enough. However, the number of possible outcomes quickly rises, and the testing problem becomes immense in the case of systems claiming true expert-level performance.

System complexity is not unique to expert systems. There are many complex information processing systems without expert system components. These are tested by testing each module of code separately and then by combining modules and testing the system as it is put together. The need for structure in large expert systems cannot be understated. Without this ability to carry out unit testing, the maintenance problem quickly gets out of hand. This is confirmed by the experience of DEC with XCON described in the next section.

The lack of absolute solutions is a more fundamental problem. It represents a barrier to the use of some techniques which are employed in other complex information systems. Consider, for example, the use of parallel software development in safety critical areas.

The European aerospace manufacturers have pioneered the so-called 'fly-by-wire' technique in civil airliners. In such planes, the computers fly the aircraft. It is clearly vital that no errors reach the flying mechanisms of the plane. There has been much debate about whether such a complex information system can ever be guaranteed 100% error-free. In order to alleviate such fears, the computer system is based around five separate computers, each of which can fly the plane alone if required. The software is made up of two systems, each developed separately by different developers. These are constantly operated in parallel and any discrepancy is immediately apparent.

This is only possible because of the establishment of a rigid specification, so that any disagreement between the systems is clearly due to an error in one of them. The application of this idea to expert systems, employed in other safety-critical areas as well, is clearly not feasible. The prospect of flight by committee is not an attractive one. The lack of an absolute answer prevents parallel design as a safety feature. In modelling human expertise, the computer gains all the disadvantages of subjectivity. It remains to be seen whether, the advantages can outweigh them.

2.4 Good software practice

Good software is associated with a number of features. The characteristics associated with good software include reliability, maintainability, adaptability. More comprehensive models published by Boehm *et al* (1978) and McCall *et al* (1977) will be examined in Chapter 6. These virtues arise from good practice in the development stages. Many of these virtues are associated with structured programs. In the past, many expert systems have lacked structure. This is fine for the simple shell-based systems. However, larger projects require the same attention to project management as other systems. Arguably, the most widely heralded large expert system project has been R1/XCON at DEC (McDermott, 1985), used to configure VAX systems. Its success may be judged in terms of the money saved by the corporation, and by its imitators amongst other companies. The success of XCON may be attributed to a number of factors:

(a) XCON has always had a project team associated with it for maintenance and modification. It is been an evolving project.

(b) XCON has grown to a system of *ca.* 5,000 rules. It has components in 5 different languages. The need for structuring such a system has been stressed (McDermott(*ibid*)).

(c) XCON was subject to a major rewrite at the point where the structure was starting to break down due to incremental development.

(d) The investment in support for XCON is extensive. It is suggested that this figure has been justified not simply in terms of savings in configuring systems, but also in kudos for the DEC corporation.

The management of a large expert systems project shows many similarities to any other software project. Traditional 'good practice' from software engineering should not be ignored, simply because the system is manipulating knowledge rather than information. Part of the integration process is to take into account lessons that have been learnt in the management of other large software projects.

Three lessons, at least, may be drawn from experience in large information system development projects, and applied to the development of large expert systems. Learning these lessons will contribute to the design and implementation of systems that embody the virtues that software engineers regard as characteristic of good systems.

The need for the right team. Walters and Nielsen (1988) suggest that the following are key members of the team. A project champion to facilitate the project within the organization and provide channels of communication, both inside and outside the project team. A project leader who is in charge of keeping the project on target and schedule. It may be difficult to find a leader who is experienced in both expert systems and project management. An assistant should be appointed, who is perhaps less experienced in project management, but is able to advise the leader on issues arising from the expert systems aspects of the work. It is suggested that the knowledge engineeringrole be taken typically by four people: two experienced knowledge engineers and two apprentices who are trained on the job, gradually taking a larger role, and being responsible for project maintenance.

The need for the right development methodology. We shall consider system development methodologies in Chapter 4. The right methodology is vital to the project, and the needs of systems with a large expert systems content may not be well suited to methodologies based upon rigid problem specification at the start.

The need for the right problem In the past, those systems which have succeeded have often done so because of the nature of the problem, which maps well onto the strengths and weaknesses of expert systems. This is unsatisfactory for the problem-solver, who wishes to be able to solve a specific problem by the most effective means available. The approach presented in the following chapters is to target the expert system components to those parts of the problem best suited to this kind of solution, and leave the number crunching to numeric processing. In this way, the additional problems associated with expert systems can be limited, and will only be encountered when absolutely necessary.

This approach of targeting expert systems at the most desirable sections of a problem is examined in the next chapter.

2.5 Further reading

A good introduction to the process of knowledge acquisition for expert systems, with some good examples and illustrations:
Hart, A. (1989) *Knowledge Acquisition For Expert Systems,* 2nd edn., Chapman Hall.

The experience of DEC with R1/XCON is a good grounding for anyone interested in large expert systems projects :
McDermott, J. (1985) *Doing R1 with style,* 2nd conference on AI appl., Miami.

A good survey of knowledge representation schemes is to be found in Part III of this book:
Walters, J.R. and Nielsen, N.R. (1988) *Crafting Knowledge-Based Systems,* Wiley, New York.

One of the best regarded standard texts about PROLOG. However, it is worth noting that some of the most popular PROLOG compilers show considerable departures from standard PROLOG, and if you wish to use one of these it may be necessary to investigate a book about that specific dialect:
Clocksin, W. F. and Mellish, C. S. (1987) *Programming in PROLOG* (3rd edn), Springer-Verlag, N.Y.

A good text with lots of worked examples. The book assumes a knowledge of Turbo Pascal up to v.5.0 :
Shammas,N. (1989) *Object-Oriented Programming with Turbo Pascal,* Wiley, New York.

Called a C + + primer, the book assumes a ground level knowledge of standard C:
Lippman, S. B. (1989) *A C + + Primer,* Addison-Wesley.

The aims of integrating expert systems into mainstream software

The conventional information system stops short of making judgements. It manipulates data and provides correct solutions to problems based upon data presented to it. However, there are some problems where this is inadequate. Such problems require judgement in situations where there are no correct solutions, merely degrees of correctness. These problems may be soluble by expert systems. At the same time, judged by conventional standards, expert systems are very often slow, complex and unreliable. Integration aims to combine the best of both worlds, combining more traditional software virtues with greater flexibility in problem-solving. In doing so, the concept of expert systems as 'artificial intelligence' may be unhelpful.

In this chapter, expert systems are described in terms of extending the range and capabilities of computer systems, rather than as surrogate human experts . The different approaches to integrating expert systems are introduced and the advantages and disadvantages of these approaches are discussed.

3.1. Views of expert systems

3.1.1 Expert systems as artificial intelligence?

We have already seen that expert systems have developed out of the ideal of 'artificial intelligence'. Further, we have seen that they show some limitations and characteristics which are a result of their separate development from mainstream software engineering. Viewed as information system, they are often slow, unreliable, difficult to maintain and lacking in usability. A plausible explanation for this is that expert systems are not viewed as a form of information system, but as a substitute for a human expert, a step on the road to the ideal of 'artificial intelligence'. The view of expert systems as a surrogate human expert faces major problems. The expert system is supposed to match or even exceed human performance, but in a number of key areas, it fails dismally in nearly all cases:

(a) Learning. Learning is a key component of intelligent behaviour. The subject of machine learning is a controversial one. Great claims have been made for learning by induction (Michie and Johnson, 1985), a process by which a set of rules is derived from a set of examples. However, these claims may be treated with caution for a number of reasons. The same successful examples are frequently quoted, suggesting that the number of successful cases is small. But a more controversial area concerns defining the safe limits of a system derived from induction. Consider

the situation illustrated in Fig. 3.1. If we represent a system as a complex relationship between two parameters 'muchness' and 'manyness', then specific examples provide us with a number of discrete points where that relationship is defined. Induction provides a means of extrapolating the relationship, to define a continuous relationship shown as a dashed line between the specific points defined by the examples. It does not tell us what goes on outside of the range of examples given, nor does it tells us the accuracy of the model derived, which depends upon the number and quality of examples used. In practice, the relationships represented will be multidimensional, not simply two dimensional, but this seems likely only to exacerbate the problem.

Even if one were to succeed in providing a system which could learn, the maintenance problems would appear to be insurmountable. Imagine trying to maintain 100 systems which all started from the same position one year ago, but were all self-modifying in the interim! Some of the issues raised by the possibilities of self-modifying software are examined in Partridge (1986).

(b) Monitoring Anomalies. Mention has already been made of the problems of a novice user spotting anomalous results from an expert system. Remember the million pound gas bill? Human beings are very good monitors. In relatively clean steady-state situations, computers can also be effective. However, the typical problem requiring 'artificial intelligence' is noisy and ill-defined, else it could be tackled using an algorithmic approach.

(c) Scope and Flexibility. The archetypal problem for an expert system is a narrow problem domain requiring specific and detailed domain expertise. In practice, many problems require contextual knowledge and are not suitable for expert systems. Others can be solved without resort to such knowledge 99% of the time, but 1% of the time they require a flexible response. In many applications this occurrence is the time when a correct response is vital.

(d) Intuition. Human beings do not necessarily arrive at an answer by strict direct logic. Many people will argue for the use of intuition or following hunches. This amounts to reasoning on the basis of incomplete information based upon an informal knowledge base built up from experiences in life over many years. The person concerned may not even be aware of the knowledge employed. Use is often made of experience from analogous situations, either consciously or subconsciously. These techniques, which may be summarized as informal reasoning are practically impossible to replicate in a computer system. The limitations described are summarized in Fig. 3.2.

Computers are good at being computers. Despite the best efforts of many researchers, they are still not very good at being human experts. So let's accentuate the positive by considering an alternative view of expert systems as flexible computer systems.

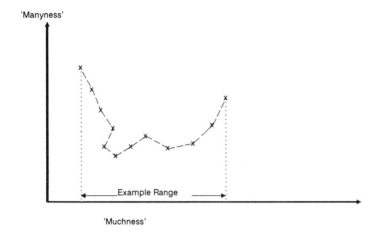

Fig. 3.1 Induction : learning from examples.

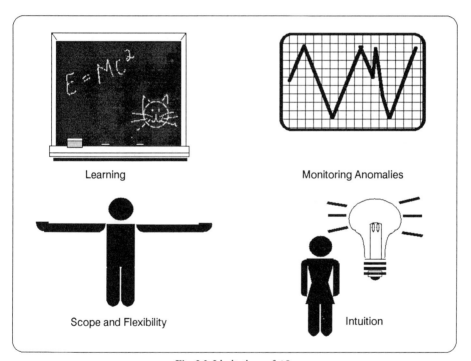

Fig. 3.2 Limitations of AI.

3.1.2 Expert systems as knowledge processing systems

The alternative view of expert systems is as computer systems with the potential to tackle some of the problems unsuited to more conventional software techniques. The characteristics of such problems which suggest that an expert solution may provide a sensible solution are:

(a) *No deterministic solution.* One where it is not possible to provide a deterministic algorithmic solution. Expert system solutions are less reliable and more expensive than algorithmic solutions, so should only be considered when such a solution is unavailable or impracticable.

(b) *Clearly defined limits.* One where, without a computer, the problem might be tackled using a limited but detailed set of knowledge. The problem should have clearly-defined limits.

(c) *Machine representable knowledge.* One where the form of available expertise is within the limits of today's knowledge representation technology. Many problems require the use of broad, contextual knowledge, which we might consider to be 'common-sense' . Such knowledge is a glaring example of one common form of knowledge which is not thus far amenable to machine representation in manageable form.

(d) *Available expertise.* One where there is a convenient source of good quality expertise. The system can only be as good as the knowledge on which it is based, and only if such expertise is available in the first instance.

In practice, many problems may have some components which require the extra flexibility of expert systems. In such a scenario, to use expert systems to solve the whole problem would be an inefficient and ineffective solution. The use of expert systems as knowledge processors within a broader IT solution enables the designer to produce systems which target the knowledge processing where they are most needed, whilst utilizing conventional information processing for the more tractable parts of the problem. This targeting approach forms the basis of the author's use of integrated expert systems, and will be discussed further in later chapters.

We must now consider what exactly is meant by an integrated expert system.

3.2 What is an integrated expert system?

In Chapter 1, we defined integration of expert systems on three levels: concept, data and coding. It has been suggested that with each level comes increasing complexity, but that this is matched by greater benefits. In practice, much of the work concerned with integrating expert systems with other technologies has been concerned with integrating Database Management Systems (DBMSs) with expert systems. The application of such systems in decision support is discussed in Chapter 9 (Case Study III). In terms of the three-level model of integration, this approach represents integration at the data level, based upon integration of the common data- and knowledge-base. The systems remain as separate entities, and this is encouraged by the desire of system designers to add expert systems to existing DBMSs. The extent to which this possible depends upon the degree of coupling between the systems. However, integration at the data level remains only a partial solution, total integration only being achieved at the coding level.

Integration at the code level may be considered in two ways: horizontally and vertically. Horizontal integration is shown in Fig. 3.3.

Horizontal integration replaces the established 'expert system' and 'information system' concepts with a continuous spectrum of possible systems. The position in the spectrum of an optimum solution should be determined by the needs of the problem. The designer aims to keep as far to the left of the spectrum as possible, in order to minimize the design constraints. The nature of the problem works against this, pushing the solution to the right of the spectrum as the needs of the problem become greater in terms of knowledge processing. The approach may, therefore, be considered to be problem-driven.

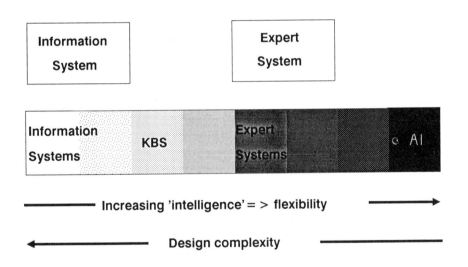

Fig. 3.3 'Horizontal' integration.

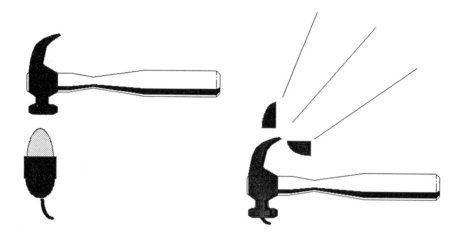

Preconceptions about the type of solution required can lead to inefficient and ineffective solutions !

Fig 3.4 The ludicrous happens in computing.

This contrasts with the scenario where the designer has preconceptions about the kind of solution that is required. The objective in this case is to build the best information system or the best expert system possible. This may be considered as technology-driven, and would seem likely that such preconceptions are unhelpful (Fig 3.4). Consider the analogy of cracking a series of nuts. A range of tools is provided from a humble nutcracker through a pair of molegrips to a hammer and finally a sledgehammer. The most efficient solution requires matching the tools to the nuts. You are unlikely to make the mistake of picking the proverbial sledge hammer to crack an acorn.

Imagine having a preconception that a sledgehammer was the best tool for all nutcracking. It is likely to produce an inefficient and ineffective solution. In our enthusiasms for expert systems, we must guard against trying to crack the metaphorical acorn (our problem) with the metaphorical sledge hammer (our expert system).

Vertical integration adds a further dimension to integration. The overall problem is divided into a series of component tasks. Each task may then be tackled using the optimum solution from within the horizontal spectrum of systems. The result may be seen as a two dimensional matrix of activities and solutions (Fig. 3.5).

To explore what this means, consider the analogy of making a chair. In order to produce the chair, we must go through a series of stages. Each stage will require its own optimum solution and have its own favoured technology. Some may even require a combination of technologies. The process of developing a chair is shown in simplified form in Tab. 3.1.

In the same way we may divide system development into a series of processes, and indeed we do. These are examined in the next chapter. For now, we must note that each process should be tackled using the most appropriate technology. Our overall solution will then consist of a number of components, each providing an optimum solution for a particular part of the problem.

3.2.1 Previous approaches to integration

Fully integrated systems represent the culmination of a number of established technologies, each representing partial integration. Three types of partially 'integrated' solutions are commonly described.

(a) Integrated DBMS/ES (information and knowledge processing). These systems have become increasingly important with the growth of database management systems, built around relational databases. They will be examined in greater detail in Chapters 5 and 8.

(b) Numerical decision support (information processing and human judgement). Statistical techniques have been used to aid decision making for a considerable length of time. The advantage of providing computerized decision support of this type is the speed and quantity of information that the computer may process reliably. In practice, statistical methods often lie at the heart of knowledge representation schemes. For example, the AI technique of 'neural networks' may be based upon a physiological metaphor, rather than the psychological metaphor at the heart of expert systems, but the technique is implemented as a sophisticated statistical network.

Alternative strategies for numerical decision support may be based around quantitative forecasting models such as regression or time series models. The principal distinction which may be drawn is the view of the world that lies at the heart of the model. In a numerical decision support system, the view is simply a numerical view. The computer takes numbers as inputs, and produces numbers as outputs. In a knowledge-based scenario, the system takes symbols as inputs, manipulates them and produces outputs and justifications in terms of these symbols.

(c) Co-operative expert systems (human and machine judgement). In order for expert systems to be effective in decision support, it is necessary for the system to be designed with co-operation in mind, and modes of co-operation must be considered at an early design phase. The co-operation model of Land and Mulhall (1989) makes this explicit in the KADS methodology. In practice, this approach is

Spectrum of possible solution types

**Problem
divided
into smaller
tasks**

| | Task 1 |
| Task 2 |
| Task 3 |
| Task 4 |
| Task 5 |

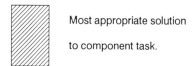

Most appropriate solution

to component task.

Fig. 3.5 Vertical integration.

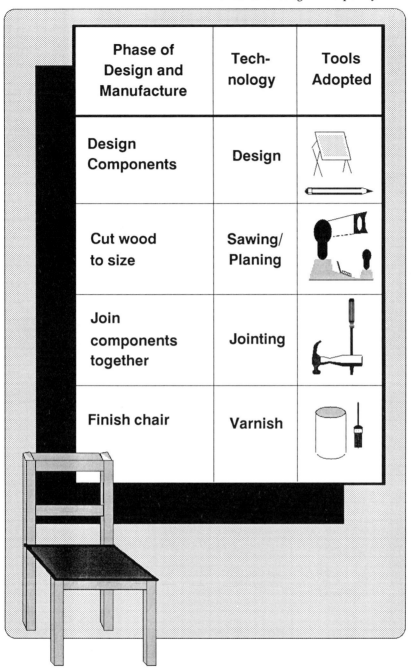

Phase of Design and Manufacture	Tech-nology	Tools Adopted
Design Components	Design	
Cut wood to size	Sawing/ Planing	
Join components together	Jointing	
Finish chair	Varnish	

Tab. 3.1 Development of a chair.

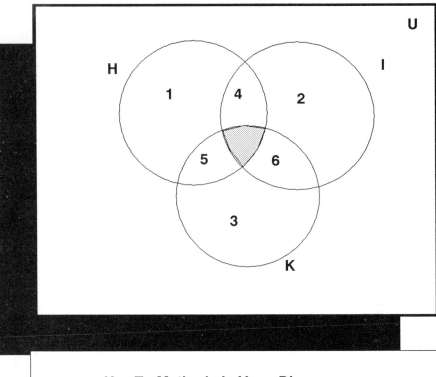

Key To Methods In Venn Diagram

1 User analysis

2 Information system

3 Archetypal stand-alone expert system

4 Numerical decision support system

5 Co-operative expert systems

6 Hybrid or hierarchical expert systems

   Fully integrated solution

Fig. 3.6 Venn Diagram representing integration.

part of a global approach to integration (Gillies and Hart, 1989a,b). However, the co-operation of user and expert system should be complemented by co-operation between information and knowledge processing if full integration is to be achieved.

Full integration may be seen as the logical culmination of other techniques. The relationship between these approaches and the central theme of full integration between the user, the computer as information processor and the computer as knowledge processor may be represented as a Venn diagram (Fig. 3.6).

Defining three sets,

I = systems based upon information processing
H = human user solution
K = systems based upon knowledge processing,

it may be seen that
$I \cap K$ represents an integrated DBMS/ES, and
$I \cap H$ represents an numerical decision support system, and
$H \cap K$ represents a co-operative expert system.
$I \cap H \cap K$ represents a fully integrated solution.

A system fully integrated at the coding level is seen as a piece of software, which conforms to the conventions of structured programming. As such it is conceived as a series of modules, each of which may be broadly classified as an information processing module or a knowledge processing module. In Chapter 5, we shall introduce the concept of a notional user module to complete the description.

3.3 Five principles for integration

Integration of expert systems is only desirable where clear benefits may be seen. The software engineer seeks integration because he believes that it will lead to the introduction of expert systems with traditional software virtues. AI designers seeks to integrate in order to show that expert systems are capable of solving problems insoluble with other techniques. The author wishes to promote integration because he believes it aids problem solving.

However, the form of integration desired is not a rigid methodology, but rather a set of ideas, from which practical methods can and will, later in the book, be devised. It is, therefore, desirable to set down the principles which lie behind integration as seen by the author.

The integration of expert systems advocated in this book is based upon five basic principles, outlined below:

3.3.1 The 'problem drives the solution' principle

Computer solutions may be judged according to two criteria:

'How good is the answer?'
'How good is the question?'

Computer systems have been improving constantly over the last decade in terms of fulfilling a specification. It is, therefore, sometimes a source of wonderment to system designers that their clients remain often unconvinced by their best efforts. The point here is that the best answer to the wrong question is still a wrong answer. In a domestic analogy, if you want a washing machine, but the shop delivers the top of the range dishwasher, then this is the wrong solution.

This is an illustration of the 'technology first' approach still prevalent amongst some system developers. They lose sight of the fact that the aim of any system is to provide a solution to a problem. They fix upon a favoured technology e.g. expert system or database management system (DBMS), and then design the best expert system or DBMS they can. They judge the end result according to whether it is a good expert system or a good database management system, not according to how well it solves a problem. In such cases, the solution drives the problem.

The 'problem drives the solution' principle states that the problem should determine the solution, and not the other way round. The effectiveness of the solution must be judged in terms of how well it solves the problem. This may require a solution which cannot be pigeon-holed easily as one type of system or another. This principle may appear self-evident. It is not always so, in the world of software development.

3.3.2 The 'means to an end' principle

The 'means to an end' principle follows from the first principle. It states that any technology, approach, tool, implementation language or hardware environment is only important as far as it contributes to the effectiveness of the overall solution to a problem. No technique or technology has a divine right to exist beyond its usefulness in contributing to a successful solution.

3.3.3 The 'toolbox' principle

The 'toolbox' principle states that the problem solver who elects to use IT to solve a particular problem has at his disposal a series of technologies, which may be likened to a set of tools within a toolbox. This is a much wider use of the term 'tool' than is conventional in computing. All technologies may be regarded as tools to assist the problem-solver in his provision of an IT solution. The problem solver's tool-box is illustrated in Fig. 3.7.

3.3.4 The 'targeting' principle

Each tool in the toolbox has a specific task for which it is designed. As a consequence, it has a range of strengths and weaknesses, which are critical to its

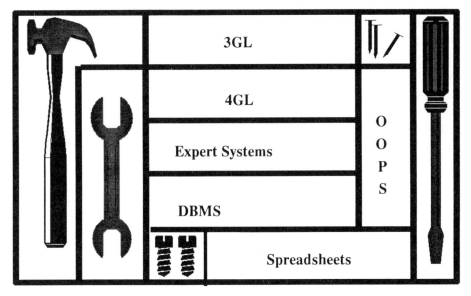

Fig.3.7 The techniques available for IT solutions.

The *'problem drives the solution' principle* states that the problem should determine the type of solution.

The *'means to an end' principle'* states that anything employed is only important as far as it contributes to the effectiveness of the overall solution to a problem.

The *'toolbox' principle* states that an IT problem solver has at his disposal a series of technologies, which may be likened to a set of tools within a toolbox.

The *targeting principle* states that an effective solution requires the targeting of each technology to the parts of the problem where it can be most effectively employed.

The *clipping principle* states that each contributing technology must only be used within its designed operating range.

Tab. 3.2 Five principles for integration.

successful employment in the search for an effective solution. The targeting principle states that an effective solution requires the targeting of each technology to the parts of the problem where it can be most effectively employed.

3.3.5 The 'clipping' principle

This is an extension of the last principle. Each tool has an operating range within which it can operate successfully. Operation outside this range may have disastrous consequences. The name is derived from the operation of amplifiers which when operated outside of their designed range are said to be driven into 'clipping'.

Thus, the clipping principle states that each contributing technology must only be used within its designed operating range. The five principles are summarized in Tab. 3.2.

3.4 The pros and cons of integrating expert systems

3.4.1 Why bother? The advantages of integration

The aim of integration is to introduce some of the advantages of conventional software engineering, whilst retaining as many of the special features of expert systems as possible. It has already been stated that expert systems have been less than enthusiastically received by the software engineering community. We shall consider a number of possible reasons and examine the advantages of integration in each case.

(a) Prejudice. It may seem a little eccentric to put prejudice at the top of our list of factors. However, illogical human factors are often more important than strict logical reasons. Prejudice and preconceptions exist in both the software engineering and AI communities. The software engineers often appear prejudiced because expert systems are different. They do not fit the preconceived software engineering ideas of how systems should be developed nor how they should be tested and they depend upon domain experts who may know nothing of computers.

The AI community also harbours its own prejudices. In the past, it has appeared that some researchers have aimed at the single objective of providing cleverer expert systems with a greater depth of symbolic reasoning. This has perpetuated the continuing development of expert systems as separate entities. These people seem to feel threatened by the prospect of integration, as if the 'black magic' of AI will be diluted and dissipated.

As usual, these prejudices are based upon a certain amount of truth. By considering integration, these concerns in both communities may be examined in a more rational way.

(b) Development. The conventional waterfall model of development, explored in the next chapter, does not suit expert system development well. However, there is growing evidence that information systems designed in this way are becoming increasingly unacceptable to their users, and the exploration of alternative

methods is not restricted to expert systems. The possibility of integration is the development of methodologies able to handle the idiosyncracies of expert systems within a disciplined approach acceptable to software engineers.

(c) Expert systems are toys. The scale of expert systems and the development of large-scale systems has always been problematical, although the classic example of DEC with XCON shows that large expert systems are possible and can be cost-effective. The advantage of integration is that it allows expert systems to be targeted at specific components, therefore, a small scale expert system can make a meaningful contribution to large scale project.

(d) Lack of software virtues. It is regrettably true that many previous expert systems have lacked the traditional software virtues of reliability, maintainability and efficiency. The problem is that these criteria have simply not been given a high enough priority in many cases. There is a 'chicken-and-egg' situation here. Many systems are developed as lab prototypes. Without the incentive of a commercial product, there is little reason to invest heavily in maintainable, reliable code. However, without these virtues, the prototype is unattractive to developers who might wish to produce that commercial product. Unreliable, unmaintainable, inefficient code should not be acceptable in any environment, be it laboratory or commercial.

(e) Testing problems. Expert systems are difficult to test because of their complexity. However, there are many complex information systems around. testing strategies developed for large-scale information systems have a potential role to play in improving the testing of expert systems, and the cross-fertilization of ideas and techniques is part of the integration process at the concept level.

(f) Dilution of the special characteristics of expert systems. The question here is 'what defines an expert system?' A system is not an expert system because it enshrines a particular language, data structure or paradigm. It is an expert system because it provides expert level performance through whatever means it can. Certainly, the use of 3GLs or other non-AI implementation media puts constraints upon the designer. However, constraints may be overcome with clever solutions e.g. case study II in Chapter 8. Furthermore, any AI representation is reduced to binary code at the fundamental machine level. This suggests that many AI representations, once devised within a specialist environment, are capable of representation in a more universal format. Integration is a challenge to the designer, but the potential benefits of circumventing the constraints in terms of the acceptability of the end system are enormous.

3.4.2 The disadvantages of integrating expert systems

Inevitably, however, there are disadvantages and problems associated with integration.

(a) Charting the unknown. Another human factor comes top of the list of problems. People like systems that can be 'pigeon-holed'. They like to know what they are getting. If we attempt to sell our integrated solution as an information system solution then we are faced with justifying a lot of additional complexity. If it is presented as an expert system, then we face all the problems outlined above.

(b) Extra complexity. An inevitable consequence of an integrated system is the additional complexity associated with the design process of the whole system and the interface between the knowledge-based and information-based components of the code.

(c) Finding a suitable design approach . Existing tools and methodologies are designed to cater for the specific characteristics of information or expert systems, but not both. A certain creativity in the use of tools and processes is required for a successful solution.

(d) Staffing a project. Staffing a project may be tricky. Personnel conversant with both information and expert systems may be scarce, and in a team situation, there is the potential for the team to divide along 'party' lines if staff are drafted in with one or other type of experience. Human nature leads us to stick to what we know. The best sort of people are those motivated by a desire to solve problems. A colleague of mine said that when he wrote his first expert system he was unaware that he had done so. Only after the system had been developed, and the problem solved, did he realize that it was an expert system. People who start like this are worth their weight in gold during the development of an integrated system.

(e) Falling between two stools. There is a danger of reducing each component system to the lowest common denominator. The desired solution is the best of all worlds. The potential worst case is the combined weaknesses of both information and expert systems without any of the benefits. This should be avoidable by careful design and a good knowledge of the respective techniques.

The pros and cons of integration are summarized in Tab. 3.3.

3.4.3 Design issues for integrated systems

An integrated system requires an approach to system development that can cope with the flexibility of expert systems but can lead to software with the qualities that have often been lacking in expert systems in the past.

The current situation in systems development is marked by a profusion of development methodologies. Most of them are targeted either at expert systems or information systems. It is not the primary intention of this book to supplement that crowded arena. Rather, in the next two chapters, we shall review existing development strategies from the viewpoint of the integrated system designer. We

Pros of integration ✓	Cons of integration ✗
Overcoming prejudices	Charting the unknown
Re-examination of development issues	No specific development path
Overcoming toy domains	Extra complexity
Overcoming lack of software virtues	Staffing a project
Addressing issues in testing	Falling between two stools
Dilution of special nature of AI	

Tab. 3.3 The pros and cons of integration.

shall consider the issues relevant to integration under the headings of software engineering, human/computer interaction and quality. Following this, the case studies aim to show how some designers have approached integration in very different problem domains. Only after this will we discuss a strategy to enable the user to develop a methodology for integrated systems.

3.5 Further reading

These two references represent opposing views of machine induction. Read them and decide....

Hart, A. E. (1987) The role of induction in knowledge elicitation, in *Knowledge Acquisition: a practical Casebook* (ed. A Kidd), Plenum Press.

Michie,D. and Johnston,R. (1985) *The creative computer,* Pelican, London.

Professor Partridge sees machine learning as an essential part of artificial intelligence systems. In his book, he considers some of the software engineering issues arising.

Partridge, D. (1986) *Artificial Intelligence: the future of software engineering,* Ellis-Horwood, Chichester.

CHAPTER FOUR

Issues in integration: software engineering

Traditionally in software engineering, a waterfall lifecycle model methodology has been adopted, based around a complete and universal specification. An expert system has no such complete specification. Thus, it is not surprising that alternative methodologies have evolved for expert systems, based upon prototyping . However, an exclusive association of prototyping with expert systems is misleading, and many methodologies combine elements of good practice from both approaches. The introduction of a new generation of CASE (Computer Aided Systems Engineering)tools to support the use of these methodologies is helping software engineers produce code more reliably and efficiently. These tools may also provide a way forward for knowledge engineers in promoting a better understanding of problems. At the same time, specialist AI tools such as KEE or ART are emerging to make prototyping and implementation of systems easier. Creative use of a range of tools may yet be required to produce systems integrated at the code level.

In this chapter, we shall examine the specification available for problems amenable to expert systems. We shall describe the prototyping and waterfall lifecycle model methodologies, and examine the traditional association of prototyping with expert systems and the lifecycle methodology with information systems. We shall look at how some of the emerging CASE tools and associated methodologies may help the production of integrated systems.

4.1 Historical trends in software engineering

Just as the historical development of expert systems from AI has determined many of the current trends and beliefs in expert systems, so a study of the historical development of software engineering can contribute to our understanding of the current situation in that discipline. Some of the key stages in the historical development of software engineering are summarized in Fig. 4.1.

Early programming occurred at the machine code level and employed directly the code used by the machine itself. Ever since then, languages have been developed which have been moving steadily further away from the machine code itself. Third generation languages (3GLs) such as Pascal, FORTRAN, COBOL, C and ADA have now been joined by 4GLs such as Ingres, Focus and Powerhouse and Telon, which it is claimed are easier to use and hence lead to more structured programs and higher programmer productivity.

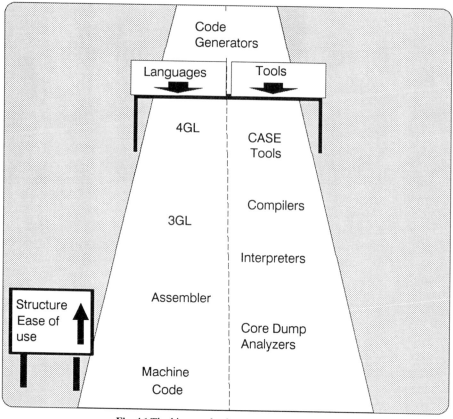

Fig. 4.1 The history of software engineering tools.

Accompanying these developments have been a series of tools which have aided the programming function. The first tools were simple translators to turn the source code into machine code. These gave way to compilers which in addition to translation provided a degree of error checking. These have been accompanied by increasingly sophisticated debugging tools. All these tools are associated with the implementation phase of the development process. The next stage of tool development is concerned with supporting the design stages of the development cycle. These are the current generation of CASE tools, described in more detail shortly. The next generation of CASE tools are likely to incorporate code generators to transform the system designs automatically into code. The divide between languages and tools is getting harder to spot all the time e.g. Telon is variously described as a language, a lower CASE tool and an application generator.

The driving force behind these developments has been the desire for higher quality software at lower cost. The trends in languages and tools has been accompanied by the growth of methodologies to instruct people how to program correctly. Some of these are considered in the next section.

In mainstream software, many early systems were poorly written and this led to the appearance of 'spaghetti code', code which is not logically organized, is difficult to maintain and is consequently high cost and low quality. The reaction against this has led to the dominance of structured methods, where the problem is tightly defined at the start, then broken down into smaller logical units. Each smaller part is coded, tested and then put back together. The result is a whole where any errors can be easily isolated leading to lower maintenance costs. Easier testing means that there should be less errors to start with.

This model of software development requires the problem to be well understood and defined at the start of the project. This is rarely true with expert systems, requiring the use of less formal development methodologies. This in turn is a major source of the scepticism shown by many mainstream software engineers towards expert systems. There are, however, some voices in mainstream software who suggest that this strong emphasis on structured methods has sometimes produced very elegant solutions to the wrong problem.

The integration of expert systems requires a re-assessment of some widely-held beliefs in software engineering, particularly the emphasis on structured sequential development methodologies. However, it may be that the results of that re-assessment may be felt beyond the confines of integrated expert systems, and that greater emphasis will be placed upon making sure the solution solves the problem as posed.

4.2 Prototyping vs classical waterfall lifecycle methodology

4.2.1 What is a methodology?

The term 'methodology' has passed into computing jargonese: it means literally the study of the way of doing something. In computing terms, it has come to mean a systematic framework for the development of systems. In practice, it is often incorrectly used synonomously with the word 'method'. A methodology is notoriously difficult to define simply, but here's our working definition:

'A methodology is a framework for the systematic organization of a collection of methods.'

Once again, in providing a concise definition, we are sacrificing universality. By way of expansion, let's consider some of the properties of a methodology, as described by Lantz (1989):

It can be taught. A methodology involves a collection of methods. They may be ordered as a sequence of steps, and the nature and order of each step may be taught.

It can be scheduled. The time and resources required to complete each stage may be estimated, and a project schedule drawn up accordingly.

It can be measured. This schedule may be used to measure progress of the plan.

It can be compared. The use of the methodology within a specific project may be compared with its use in another project, or with the use of another methodology.

It can be modified in the light of experience.

Information System Development (ISD) methodologies used in system development, are just one class of methodology and in addition to the inherited general properties, have properties of their own. The examples shown in the Venn diagram (Fig. 4.2) are SSADM (Structured systems analysis and design methodology), IEM (Information engineering methodology) and JSP (Jackson structured programming).

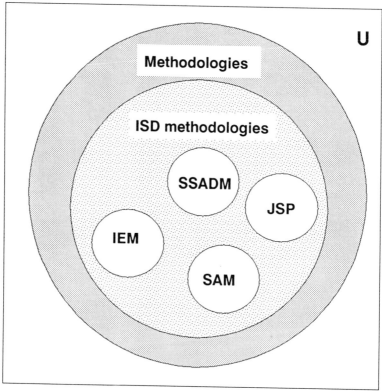

Fig. 4.2 Methodologies.

Each has been designed with its own purpose in mind, and has a blend of strengths and weaknesses as a consequence. However, a good ISD methodology should show certain common properties.

(a) Usability. It should be easy to use and have good support provided by the vendor, since this is just as important to the long-term usability of the product.

(b) Integrity. A methodology should provide coverage of the whole lifecycle to ensure integrity throughout the process.

(c) Adaptability to local needs. Methodologies are necessarily restrictive if they are to encourage good practice, but they should also be adaptable to the needs of a particular environment.

(d) Clarity. Documentation is a critical and often neglected area. Good documentation can be facilitated by the methodology and partly generated by associated tools. The methodology itself should be jargon-free and produce understandable output.

(e) Automation. Increasingly, methodologies are becoming automated through the use of tools. A good methodology should lend itself to automation.

The steps in a typical development methodology would be

Feasibility Study
Requirements Definition
Design
Coding
Unit testing
Acceptance testing
Training
Conversion from old system
Installation

Different projects have had different needs, leading to a variety of methodologies. Each of these emphasizes different aspects of software development. Methodologies have also tended to develop as a response to, and as a reaction against, the limitations of existing methodologies.

The two broad classes of development methodologies, which will be familiar to software engineers are the waterfall lifecycle methodology and the prototyping methodology.

4.2.2 Methodologies based upon the waterfall lifecycle

Sommerville (1989) identifies five phases in the waterfall lifecycle: requirements analysis, system and software design, implementation, testing and operation and maintenance. They are illustrated in Fig. 4.3.

(a) Requirements analysis. The aims, objectives and limits of the system are established in consultation with the client. They must be defined in a way that is understandable to the client and detailed enough for development staff.

(b) System and Software Design. The requirements analysis is used to allocate tasks to either hardware or software systems. Software design is concerned with transforming the software requirements into a form suitable for representation as a program.

(c) Implementation and Unit testing. This section is concerned with coding. It is the stage when the program is actually built.

(d) Testing. Testing occurs in three phases, unit testing, system testing and acceptance testing. First each unit is tested to ensure that it functions and conforms to its specification. Following unit testing, the units are combined to

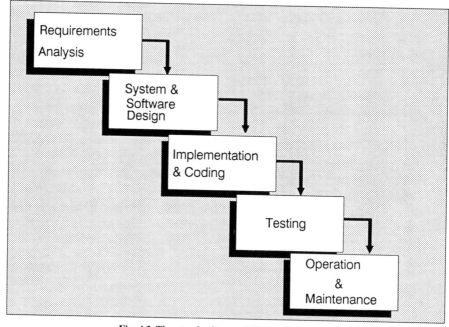

Fig. 4.3 The standard 'waterfall' lifecycle model.

form a whole system, and the completed system is tested to ensure that it performs according to the overall specification. Finally, the system is shown to the users to test to ensure that it meets their requirements. In practice this is often done as part of the installation and operation phase.

(e) *Operation and maintenance.* The product is installed and used by the client. Maintenance is ongoing, concerned not just with 'bug-fixes' but improving the product and answering new user requirements as they emerge.

The stereotyped view of such design procedures is of a series of distinct phases, each performed sequentially, each completely documented and 'signed off' as agreed with the client at the end of each phase. The practical consequence of this is that once the requirements analysis determines the specification, it is cast in stone and nothing may depart from it. Unfortunately, most problems do not permit a complete and accurate specification at the start of the project. As the project progresses, the problem will become better understood, and changes to the specification may be beneficial. Rigid adherence to the original specification is likely to ensure high technical quality e.g. maintainability and reliability, at the risk of not matching the client's needs.

In practice, a degree of iteration is often employed, the later stages shedding light on the shortcomings of the initial requirements analysis. Clearly, there is a need to ensure that consistency is maintained in such instances and tools may prove helpful in achieving this. In many projects, the degree of iteration is limited by the need to meet a deadline for that particular project phase, rather than by the reaching of a particular standard of product quality.

4.2.3 Methodologies based upon the prototyping approach

It is often observed by exasperated programmers that clients are better able to say what they don't want than define what they do. The situation is not unlike buying a birthday present for a relative. 'What would you like for your birthday?' may elicit the response 'Oh, I don't mind', but a specific question such as 'How about a book?' is likely to produce 'Well, I don't get much time to read... '. Further attempts such as ' How about some clothes?' may produce equally negative responses, for example 'Well, I don't know if it will fit ... I never like clothes that other people buy me'. Sure enough, if clothes are bought, they are just the wrong shade of pink to go with a favourite pair of shoes. Presenting the client with a possible solution focuses their attention to detailed considerations vital to the acceptability of the product.

A methodology based upon the waterfall lifecycle can lead to a correct solution to the wrong problem, if the specification is drawn up before the problem is completely understood. In prototyping methodologies, the development process defines the specification as the project progresses. The user is provided with prototype systems to allow them to say 'That's not what I meant' before the specification is finalized.

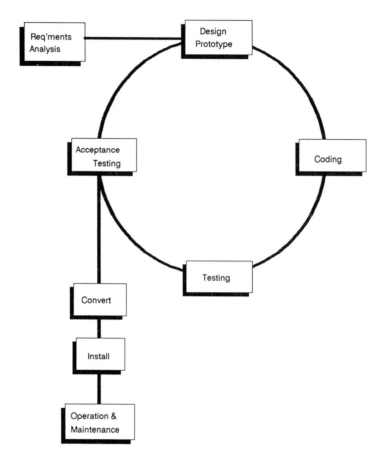

Fig. 4.4 A methodology based upon prototyping.

A typical prototyping methodology is illustrated in Fig. 4.4.
The advantages claimed for prototyping methodologies are:
- User involvement increases user satisfaction
- Reduces errors in specification
- Improves communication

One of the biggest problems with prototyping methodologies is the issue of 'adequacy', or in simple terms, 'When do we stop?' We shall consider this question when we consider such methodologies in detail.

One of the problems faced by 'expert systems' in the past has been its association with prototyping methodologies which do not carry the credibility of sequential, waterfall-based methodologies in software engineering circles. I shall aim to show why this association has arisen, and how practical methodologies must combine elements of both 'waterfall' and 'prototyping' methodologies.

4.3 Defining the problem: the need for a complete specification

4.3.1 Problem definition for expert systems

In any information system, defining the specification can be a problem, particularly at the start of the project, during the initial requirements analysis. This has led to the relaxing of the rigid waterfall methodology, and the growth of prototyping methodologies. The specific difficulty associated with knowledge-based systems is the comparative ignorance of the knowledge engineer at the start of the project and consequently the important role of knowledge acquisition. In a conventional project, it is assumed that the task of drawing up the specification is about defining the problem. At the start of a knowledge-based system project it is not clear whether the knowledge required can be captured and arranged in a suitable form for system implementation. This will only emerge at the knowledge representation stage. Yet the knowledge engineer needs a project specification to define the limits of the knowledge elicitation exercise. The need for a flexible, evolving specification is, therefore, enshrined in the development process.

An initial set of provisional requirements is needed at the start of the project, and these have to be based upon management and users perception of the project requirements. It is then up to the project developers to evaluate the realism of these perceived objectives through some form of feasibility study. The feasibility study needs to address three types of issues:

(a) Technical Issues
Is there a feasible algorithmic solution?
Is the knowledge required representable on a machine?
Is the expertise accessible?
Who are the intended users, and what user model is required?

(b) Economic Issues
What is the likely cost to the organization?
What are the potential benefits?
What is the risk of failure?

(c) Organizational Issues
Is the organization amenable to new technologies?
What training requirements are there?
What are the organizational implications for structure and practices?

Given the comparative ignorance of the development team regarding the problem domain, it appears that the answers to many of these questions will only be found as the project proceeds. This leads inevitably to some form of prototyping methodology. However, a number of development methodologies have arisen which attempt to exploit the advantages of prototyping whilst retaining as much of the discipline of a waterfall methodology as possible.

In practice, the rigid division of methodologies along the lines of waterfall and prototyping is a false one. There is a spectrum of methodologies spanning the whole range between the two extremes. The properties of expert systems force designers to introduce a degree of flexibility, but the amount of freedom required varies according to the specific project. Similarly amongst other information system projects, the degree of iteration within the waterfall approach will vary enormously.

4.3.2 RUDE-based methodologies for expert system development

The most common type of methodology associated with expert system development is generally referred to as the RUDE (**R**un **U**nderstand **D**ebug **E**dit) cycle. The acronym refers to the a cyclic process derived from prototyping, which it is generally accepted is required in order to firm up the specification for an expert system. It does not stand alone, as it is a cycle and therefore requires entry and exit points (Fig. 4.5).

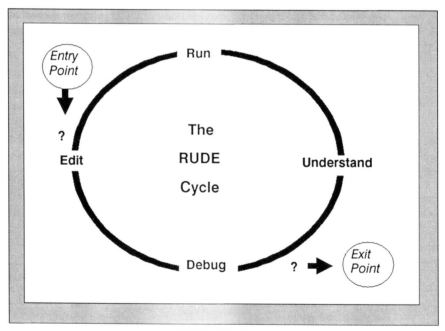

Fig. 4.5 The R.U.D.E. cycle.

As a consequence, it is incorporated not into a single methodology but rather a class of methodologies, which employ the iterative cycle to achieve different ends.

The first possible type of development methodology for expert systems uses the RUDE cycle to develop the system itself. Such a methodology is based upon traditional prototyping, described by Lantz (1989). This represents a formalization of much of the existing practice in expert systems, which employ shells to provide a medium for rapid prototyping. Such an approach can lead to a number of problems. First, an emphasis on user requirements, whilst healthy, can lead to neglect of other important characteristics. Our end product must perform satisfactorily in terms of technical quality parameters as well as fit the user's needs. Secondly, the only specification produced is the end code. This is a dubious foundation for future maintenance, and may prove costly in the longer term. This will be particularly problematical where the code itself is likely to be unstructured as a result of ill-disciplined incremental development. The third problem lies in the fact that the best medium for prototyping is unlikely to be the best medium for implementation and vice versa.

These problems are likely to be less severe for small short-lived systems, hence the popularity of shells in the development of such systems. However, they tend to confirm all the worst prejudices of the average software engineer who is concerned with larger projects and with the cost of software maintenance. The principal alternative is to use the RUDE cycle to extend the requirements phase of a more traditional software development lifecycle. This investment of resources makes sense in terms of reducing timescales, expensive mistakes and maintenance costs later in the lifecycle. It addresses the problem specification issues within the

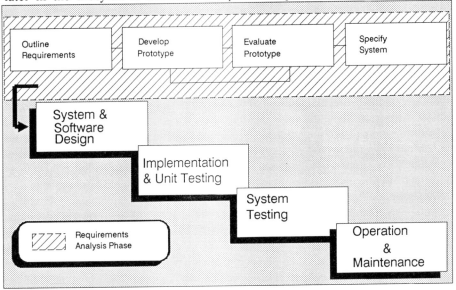

Fig. 4.6 The use of RUDE to specify a problem.

waterfall model. The stages required in such a methodology are illustrated in Fig. 4.6.

This approach can bring many of the advantages of full prototyping such as the refinement of the typically ill-defined requirements available at the start of an expert system project. It is likely to lead to an improvement of communication between all involved parties, e.g. client, domain expert and system developers, showing up the gaps in the initial analysis. It provides a working, if limited system at an early stage of the project, which may well help convince the client of the benefits of the project.

It shows advantages over full prototyping. In particular, it allows the use of an optimized medium for prototyping, yet allows a different language to be used for implementation. Thus a prototype can be implemented in a shell, an object-oriented environment such as SmallTalk, a specialist language such as LISP or PROLOG, or an advanced AI toolkit such as KEE or ART.

It also brings with it the ease of testing and documentation associated with the waterfall model. There are, as always, a number of potential pitfalls with this approach.

(a) *The Scaling Problem.* It is tempting to fall into the scaling trap, where a prototype is unrealistic because it fails to model the true depth of the problem, leading to problems in later development. Any prototype must reflect the required scale and depth of the ultimate system.

(b) *Length of the Requirements Phase.* The requirements analysis will be considerably lengthened, and this leads to increased costs in the short term.

(c) *Cost-Benefit Analysis.* The client must be persuaded of the benefits in terms of reduced maintenance costs later in the lifecycle, in order to offset the costs associated with prototype development. The benefits of this approach are greatest with larger long-term projects. A cost-benefit analysis is required early on to ensure that the investment is justified.

The prototype will not take as long to develop as a final application, since it does not require the incorporation of software standards and rigorous testing stages of the final project. Two areas where compromise is not recommended are the user interface and the depth of symbolic reasoning, since errors here can have a critical effect upon the final application.

It has been suggested that time and resources be saved by using the prototype either as the system specification itself or as the basis for the final implementation. Neither of these is in the spirit of this approach, since both compromise the principal aim, which is to combine the benefits of a rigid specification with the use of prototyping to define the problem more clearly. In expert system terms, the use of prototyping in the requirements phase represents the extension of knowledge elicitation, rather than use of prototyping for implementation. Thus the

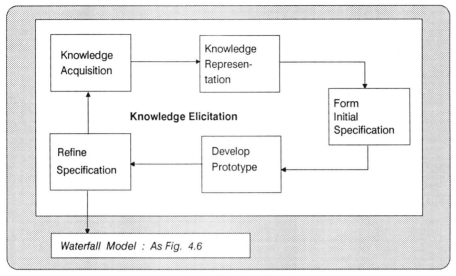

Fig. 4.7 Knowledge elicitation of requirements.

requirements analysis phase of the standard waterfall model becomes an extended knowledge elicitation phase (Fig. 4.7).

The methodologies described thus far have addressed the issue of refining the requirements of an expert system to the point where it is possible to implement a structured maintainable system. Prototyping is one technique available to us. It does not, however, assist in the production of information and expert systems integrated at the code level. One alternative strategy is to make use of tools, particularly the emerging CASE tools and AI toolkits.

4.4 The use of tools

Two classes of tools have come to the fore recently, which may be helpful to us in the development of integrated systems. They are the CASE tools, and the AI toolkits.

4.4.1 CASE tools: what can they offer?

CASE tools are computer-based tools to assist in the software engineering process. In practice, any CASE tool is made up of a set of tools or 'toolkit'.

CASE is, at the time of writing, one of the 'hot' areas of IT. It occupies a position held by expert systems a few years ago. CASE tools are being heavily promoted by suppliers and willingly bought by users. Whilst they clearly have benefits, it remains to be seen whether this period of enthusiasm will be followed by a backlash or continued euphoria. The claimed benefits for CASE tools include:

(a) Productivity. Good system developers are scarce, and the aim of these tools is to maximize productivity.

(b) Consistency. These tools provide a central data encyclopedia to which all developers must refer. It enables several developers working separately to maintain consistency in terms of variables, data, syntax and so on. In large software projects, this can justify the use of tools alone.

(c) Methodology Automation. Many tools are associated with an underlying methodology. The tool ensures that the developer sticks to the methodology. This improves consistency, but restricts creativity.

(d) Encourages Good Practice. Provided the underlying methodology is sound, the tool ensures that good practice such as structured programming is carried out.

(e) Documentation. This is a notoriously undervalued area of system development. Tools can provide degrees of automation of documentation to assist in this process.

(f) Maintenance. The principal driving force behind the introduction of CASE tools has the been the cost of maintenance. Tools can help improve initial quality, and make changes cheaper to implement.

The toolsets within a CASE tool are bound to a central data encyclopedia which maintains consistency across different component tools (Fig. 4.8). It is this

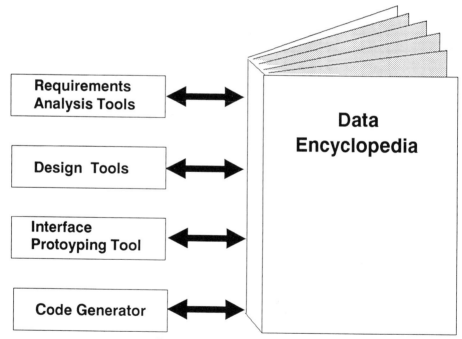

Fig. 4.8 CASE tools (Schematic).

consistency which gives CASE tools much of their value, especially in large projects.

   CASE tools are divided into three types. The classification is based upon the part of the development cycle supported by the tool concerned.

Front End or Upper CASE tools. These tools are concerned with the design phases of the lifecycle. Their purpose is to assist in requirements analysis and design. They may be tied to a specific methodology or may allow the use of the user's own methodology. An example of this type of tool is the Excelerator product, described below.

Back End or Lower CASE tools. These tools are concerned with the implementation stages of the lifecycle, typically coding testing and documentation. They aim to increase the reliability, adaptability and productivity of the delivered code. 4GLs may be considered as back end CASE tools, also products such as Telon.

Integrated CASE tools. Integrated CASE (ICASE) tools aim to support the whole development cycle. They are linked to specific methodologies. They are often complex and expensive, but offer the developer the greatest integrity of all approaches through the use of a single data encyclopedia throughout the lifecycle. An example of this type of tool is IEF.

The relationship between the different types of tools and the development lifecycle is shown in Fig. 4.9.

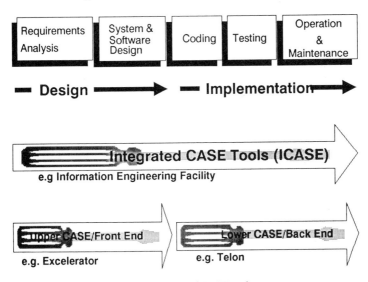

Fig. 4.9 Types of CASE tool.

For the purposes of designing integrated expert systems, we are particularly interested in tools and techniques aimed at supporting the design phase. The aim of this phase of system design is to capture the user's requirements and to incorporate them into an implementable design. This process may be tackled by building a data model using techniques such as data flow diagrams and entity relationship models. One of the standard methodologies available for system design is the structured analysis methodology, due to DeMarco and Yourdon (DeMarco, 1979).

4.4.2 Yourdon/deMarco structured analysis methodology

This methodology uses a top-down approach to system design. Put simply, it breaks the problem down into smaller, more manageable bits. This is achieved by functional decomposition, producing a structured system requirement in the form of a partitioned model of the final system. The methodology is summarized in Fig. 4.10, together with some of the principal associated techniques. The methodology

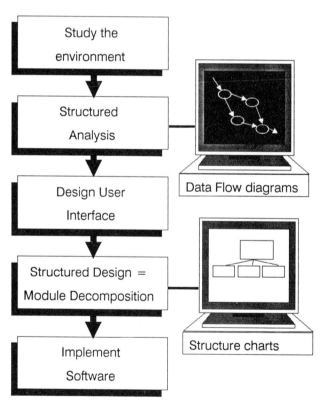

Fig. 4.10 Structured analysis methodology (SAM).

is based upon three principal techniques: data flow diagrams, mini-specifications and structure charts.

(a) Data flow diagrams. A data flow is an individual item of data. This is considered to be transmitted from one process to another. Data starts from a data source and ends at a data sink. An example of a source or sink is a human being or a machine component. A process may require data from an external file or database. This is represented as two horizontal lines. In practice, data flow diagrams are multilevel, and lend themselves to computerization, since graphical software can aid both design and understanding. Each level gives a more detailed representation than the one above. The elements in a data flow diagram are shown in Fig. 4.11, and an example of a multilevel dataflow diagram is given in Fig. 4.12.

(b) Mini-specifications. Associated with each process node at the bottom of a dataflow diagram is a task which may be described by a mini-specification, more commonly known as a mini-spec. Mini-specs describe their task in terms of algorithms which may be represented in a number of ways e.g. pseudo-code, flow-charts, computer design language, decision trees or a decision table. These mini-specifications are designed to be translated into code subroutines, either automatically by the CASE tool or manually by the programmer. A mini-spec will typically include a process name and number, an input data list, an output data list and the body of the algorithm whose purpose is to transform the input data into the output data.

(c) Structure charts. Structure charts are designed to turn the requirements specification into a design specification. A structure chart represents the design specification in terms of modules and the data paths between them (Fig. 4.13)

Each module should be simple and self-contained. The programmer seeks to minimize coupling between modules, and maximize cohesion, i.e. the degree to which a module contains all the code required to carry out its function. Some CASE tools offer the facility to transform the data flow diagram into a series of modules in the form of a structure chart.

The structured analysis methodology has been around for a number of years now, and has evolved in a number of areas. Initially, little attention was paid to user interfaces, yet they are one of the principal influences upon user satisfaction. In theory, interfaces should vary enormously according to the level of expertise of the user. In practice, they are often designed like a ready-to-wear suit of clothes: they don't fit anyone very well, but neither do they mismatch people totally. In practice, there is little methodological basis for interface design beyond certain basic ground rules. However, the interface design is now a recognized stage within the structured analysis process. Interface prototyping tools are generally tailored drawing packages, allowing the user of the tool to create interfaces rapidly.

An example of a CASE tool based upon the structured analysis methodology is the front end tool Excelerator, from the Index Technology Corporation. The

Notation used in Data Flow Diagrams

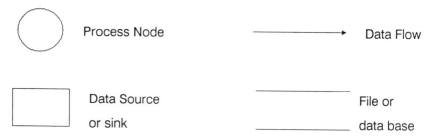

Process Node

Data Flow

Data Source
or sink

File or
data base

Fig. 4.11 Notation used in a data flow diagram.

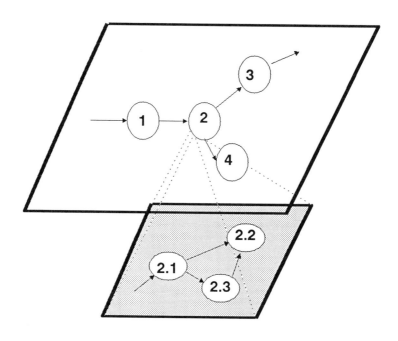

Fig. 4.12 A data-flow diagram (after Fisher).

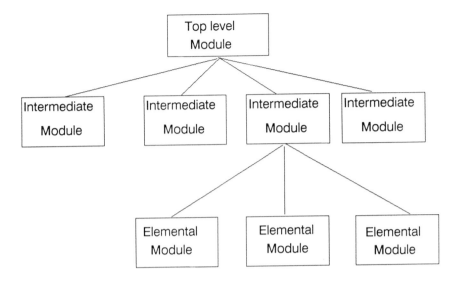

Fig. 4.13 An example structure chart.

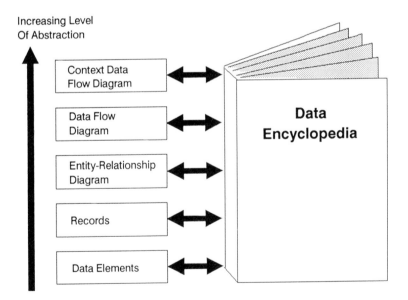

Fig. 4.14 The Excelerator CASE tool.

product is based around a set of diagramming tools supporting five levels of representation of the design (Fig. 4.14).

The product integrates the Yourdon/DeMarco Structured Analysis Methodology with data modelling and structured design methodologies. The top-level of the multi-level data flow diagram is known as the context data flow diagram and provides an overview of the whole system. The remaining techniques provide more detailed information as the levels are descended.

In addition to the diagramming tools, Excelerator offers a number of facilities to assist the designer. A screens and reports facility allows the designer to set up mock-ups of inputs and outputs for interface prototyping. Outline COBOL code may be generated automatically using a separate product. Whilst this is not implementable COBOL, it provides a good outline, from which programmers can work.

An alternative and complimentary approach to data modelling is found in the information engineering methodology supported by the IEF CASE tool. Information engineering makes extensive use of entity-relationship (E-R) models for information modelling, which attempts to model both data structures and their interrelationships. E-R models are attractive because of their simplicity. They contain only two elements: entities and the relationships between them. Entities are the objects or data structures under description. They may be specific real objects such as people or machinery, or abstract concepts such as services. The relationships between them are classified into a number of types, according to the number of entities involved. Commonly, one-to-one, one-to-many and many-to-many relationships are defined, but these are complicated by the possibility that a relationship to zero is also possible in some cases.

Consider the following example of an E-R diagram (Fig. 4.15), which forms part of the data structure for a computerized database of customer records at a newsagent's shop. The diagram employs Martin's notation as used within the IEF CASE tool.

Each customer lives at a single address. We shall not consider the possibility that the newsagent might have two customers in the same household. This means that 'customer' and 'house no.' are entities within our data model and have a one-to-one relationship. A street is made up many houses. Therefore 'street' is an entity and is linked by a one-to-many relationship to houses.

Each customer is assumed to have at least a daily paper order. They may order more than one daily paper, and each paper will be ordered by more than one customer. Therefore, the relationship between the entity 'customer' and the entity 'daily paper' is a many-to-many relationship.

Similarly, each customer may or may not have at least a weekly magazine order. They may order zero, one or more weekly magazines which may have to be delivered on more than one day of the week. Each magazine may be ordered by zero, one or many customers. Therefore, the relationship between the entity 'customer' and the entity 'weekly magazine' is a zero-or-many-to-zero-or-many

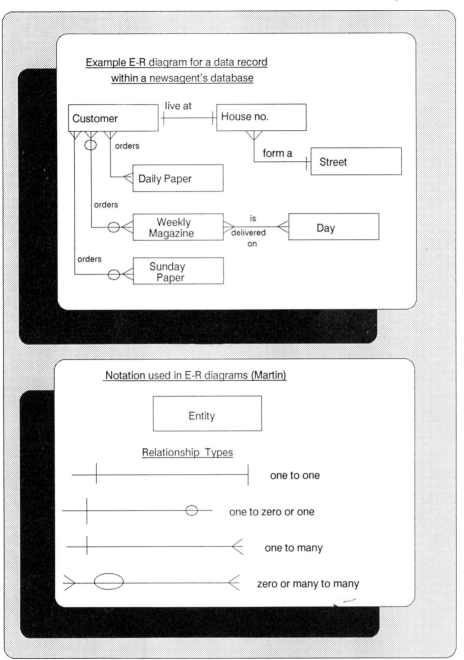

Fig. 4.15 Entity-relationship diagrams.

relationship. The relationship between the entity 'weekly magazine' and the entity 'day' is a 'many-to-many' relationship.

Finally, each customer may order zero, one or more Sunday papers. Each paper is likely to be ordered by more than one customer, so the relationship between the entity 'customer' and the entity 'Sunday paper' is a 'many-to-zero-or-many' relationship.

The use of data modelling techniques whether manual through the use of methodologies or automated through the use of CASE tools can significantly assist in the design of data rich systems. They are particularly significant in the design of expert database systems, but can prove helpful in the design of information processing components of any integrated system.

4.4.3 AI toolkits

We have already seen how shells can be used to produce simple systems, and the drawbacks associated with them. They have achieved popularity with many users who welcome their simplicity, but their lack of sophistication has led to dissatisfaction amongst the AI community. As a consequence, a new generation of tools has emerged, which are much more sophisticated and flexible. They do not share the underlying theoretical flaws of shells. A typical tool of this type, known as an AI toolkit, has a WIMP-based interface, provision for multitasking, debugging aids, support for RUDE based methods, and a range of knowledge representation schemes. These features are summarized in Fig. 4.16.

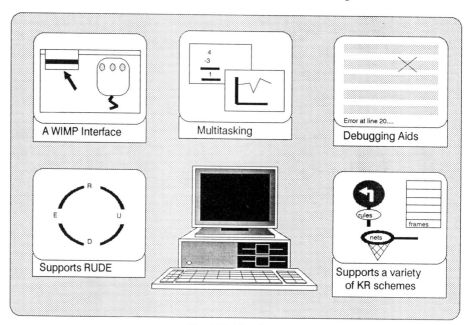

Fig. 4.16 AI toolkits.

These tools are powerful but complex and require a great deal of processing power, typically running on a workstation such as those from Symbolics or SUN. They are typically based upon the AI language LISP, and a working knowledge of LISP is helpful. They provide a rich and flexible environment for AI system design, but even on dedicated workstations, their performance is slow.

They are distinct from CASE tools in providing the data structures and paradigms required to implement symbolic reasoning rather than simple data processing.

4.5   The need for a creative use of tools

The tools described are targeted at a specific range of systems e.g. information systems or expert systems. In the case of many CASE tools, particularly integrated CASE tools, they are also tied to a specific methodology. This can limit their effectiveness for the purpose of designing integrated systems. However, in practice, many organizations are already making very selective use of CASE tools, and bearing this in mind we may also make tools selectively by targeting different tools at different parts of the problem. The use of tools in this way faces a number of problems. Apart from the heavy financial investment required, the principal problem is the lack of standards across different manufacturers. This is seen in two different ways:

(a) Notation. Even where the diagrams are representing the same model view of the problem the notation may not be identical. Consider as an example the entity-relationship diagram. Two systems are commonly found, Chen notation and Martin notation. We have used Martin's notation, as found in the IEF tool, but Chen's notation is also common.

(b) Incompatibility between output. More serious is the lack of standards to allow transfer of output from one manufacturer's tool to another. This means that the absolute integrity of a CASE tool only lasts as long as we remain within the same tool. CASE tools attempt to tie down the developer for commercial reasons to one tool. In practice this means that we are most likely to be able to make use of CASE tools at the early high-level stages of design.

The creative use of tools might be approached in the following manner. The problem may be analyzed using Yourdon's structured analysis methodology. The result from this is a partitioned problem represented as a set of modules. These modules may then be allocated to the most appropriate technology, such as expert system, information system, or perhaps user selection.

Each module may then be tackled using the best method for the job and with the assistance of the appropriate tool, an AI toolkit for the expert system, a CASE tool for the information system and an interface prototyping tool for the user

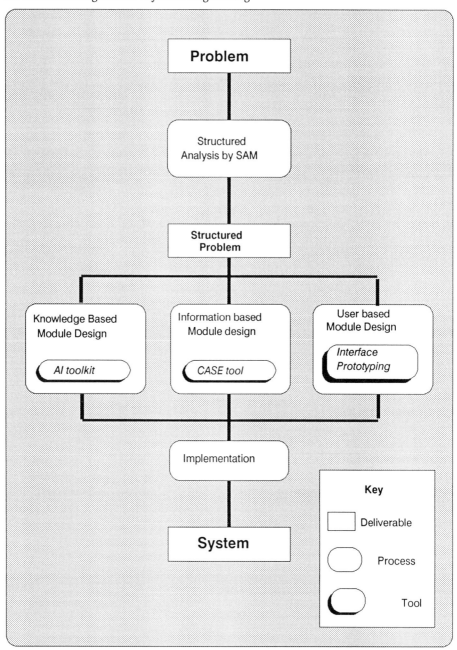

Fig. 4.17 Integrated system development framework.

modules. Once designed, the modules must then be brought back together to form a complete system.

This outline framework is summarized in Fig. 4.17. In the subsequent chapters we shall start to put some detail onto it, culminating in Chapter 10, where strategies will be proposed for the development of integrated systems within the reader's own environment.

4.6 Further reading

The Bible of structured analysis. Well written as well as essential reading:
DeMarco, T. (1979) *Structured Analysis and System Specification*, Englewood Cliffs, Yourdon Press.

This book provides a good introduction the software development process:
Sommerville, I. (1989) *Software Engineering*, 3rd edn., Addison-Wesley

A thorough description of the prototyping methodology with the bonus of a good description of what constitutes a methodology:
Lantz, K. E. (1989) *The Prototyping Methodology*, Prentice-Hall, New Jersey.

Everything you ever wanted to know about a proprietary CASE tool, but were afraid to ask!
Martin, J. (1988) *An Introduction To Information Engineering*, James Martin Associates/Texas Instruments.

This book provides a good overview of CASE tools.
It is particularly appropriate for a U.S. audience, rather than a European one. By the time this book is in print, a second edition of Fisher's text will be required due to the speed of developments in CASE technology:
Fisher, A. S. (1988) *CASE: Using Software Development Tools*, Wiley, New York.

CHAPTER FIVE

Issues in Integration: Human-Computer Interaction

Human-computer interaction (HCI) is a discipline that sits uneasily alongside the engineering aspects of software design. It is imprecise, it may be regarded as a craft, a science or as engineering, but it is ignored at the peril of the resulting system.

HCI is sometimes regarded simply as providing an attractive and useful human-computer *interface*, but is more properly the consideration of the broader issue of human-computer interaction, including the whole scope of organizational issues arising from the system.

In this chapter, we shall explore the immediate issues beyond a simple interface in terms of user modelling. We shall explore the questions, 'Who is going to use the system, and how?' Without this stage of analysis, effort down the line on sophisticated interfaces is often wasted. The archetypal scenario of an expert systems consulted by a novice user for expert advice is stereotypical and does not reflect the wider use of expert systems.

A three-agency model of interaction is described for integrated systems. The interfaces required within such a framework are investigated. Based upon this model, the issue of task allocation within an integrated system is explored.

5.1 Human-Computer Interaction: more than just a pretty interface?

Most people's first impression of a computer program is the appearance of the screen when the program is in use. The attractiveness of the screen has an important part to play in user satisfaction. This is the first level of human-computer interaction, also known as the man-machine interface. If the keyboard is unpleasant to use, if the user is required to memorize a complex set of input commands, and the output screen layout is cluttered and difficult to understand, then the program is likely to fail at the first hurdle. Users simply will not accept it.

However, if the program is easy and attractive to use, then it still may not be accepted by the user if it does not help him do his job more efficiently. Problems of this type arise if the program is inefficient or if there is a mismatch between the way the computer and the user operate. It can be something as simple as the format of reports from a database system. For example a clerk may have become very efficient over a period of time in handling a card index. If the screen layout of a replacement computerized database is laid out very differently, the clerk may be less efficient using the computerized system than with the old card index. This

First Level HCI
The man-machine interface :

Is the screen attractive ?
Do users like the program ?
Is it easy to use ?

Second Level HCI

Does the computer work
the same way as the user ?
Does it make the user more
efficient ?

Third Level HCI

How does the system fit
into the organization ?
Is overall benefit
achieved ?

Fig. 5.1 HCI classification & terminology.

second level of human-computer interaction is concerned with how effectively the program enhances the users' capabilities. Without effective interaction at this level, rejection of a superficially attractive system will occur in the longer term.

The third level of HCI occurs at the organizational level. It is the effect of introducing a computer into a human organization. There are many cases where a computer has been introduced, but little benefit has been achieved without consideration of the impact upon the organization as a whole to take advantage of the new technology. Without the benefit to the organization as a whole, the investment in the system will be wasted.

The three levels of HCI are illustrated in Fig. 5.1. In many projects, consideration of HCI is limited to the first level. In this chapter, we shall look beyond this to issues of how the user's capabilities may be enhanced by a system, and indeed how the system may be enhanced by consideration of the user's own abilities. Consideration of the third level is concerned with the management of change and is beyond the scope of this book. We shall focus upon those issues particularly relevant to integrated expert systems.

In the manufacturing arena, the user interface is considered to be of vital importance. As an example consider car design and production. Much effort goes into the design of the user interface, with consideration of everything from back support to the angle of the steering wheel. In the particular area of instrumentation displays, recent innovations have included digital and graphical displays. The use of graphical icons is well established e.g. oil warning lights, choke, indicators. Future developments are likely to include data projected onto the windscreen in front of the driver, even route information. Car manufacturers have a specific user model in mind when designing a car and the different ranges of cars available reflect this.

Contrast this with the user interface provided by the average mainframe computer system where the user is required to learn a whole series of commands for each program used. PC-based systems are sometimes a little better, but as general rule consideration of user issues is often sadly lacking in the provision of information systems, and expert systems are no exception. Where such consideration is found, it rarely runs deeper than the provision of an attractive interface as a marketing stratagem.

A lack of awareness of user issues in expert systems was noted by Berry and Broadbent (1986) and more recently in a survey by O'Neill and Morris (1989):

'user issues generally took a back seat in ES development ... Non-expert users were often the last to be considered during ES development and the MMI was tagged on at the end of the project almost as an afterthought.'

They further suggest that this may substantially affect the success of resulting systems:

'*There were again notable exceptions - some of the most successful developers involved their users at a very early stage and throughout the system development cycle*'.

Effective human-computer interaction must involve all aspects of system design, and must start at the beginning of the design process.

Within software engineering, Boehm (1981) has suggested that the cost of maintenance shows an almost logarithmic increase as the lifecycle progresses (Fig. 5.2).

Based upon the empirical evidence, it may reasonably be supposed that a qualitatively similar graph may be drawn representing the cost of rectifying errors or omissions in human-computer interaction. This cost may be assessed in terms of an 'unusability' factor (Fig. 5.3).

In a typical case where an interface is included at the end of a project, the costs arising may be very high indeed. This 'unusability' may emerge in a number of ways. In mild cases, it may be seen as a higher number of 'operator' errors. In more severe cases, it may need to be rectified by investment in training. In extreme cases, it may render the system unusable, with the associated investment wasted. Despite the obvious reluctance of companies to reveal such events, anecdotal stories of such systems abound.

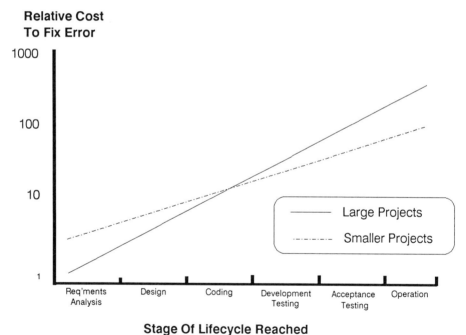

Fig. 5.2 Maintenance costs (after Boehm, 1981).

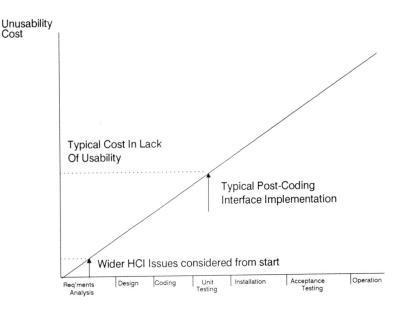

Phase of LifeCycle At Which Human factors first considered

Fig. 5.3 Costs due to 'unusability'.

Consideration of human factors at the start of the design process involves the designer in determining the answers to two fundamental questions:

'Who is going to use the system?' and 'How is it going to be used?'

The answers to these questions affect system design far beyond simple consideration of an appropriate interface.

5.1.1 Uses of Expert Systems

In the classic expert systems scenario, there are straightforward answers to the questions of who is to use the system and how it is to be used. The system is used by a novice, for consultation, in the same way as he would consult a human expert. However, in practice, systems are used in a whole variety of ways by both 'experts' and 'novices', as noted by Basden (1983). Experts may use the systems to seek a quick solution, to confirm their own judgement, for 'what if' simulations or for training. Novice users may use it for consultation, or for learning. Some of the common uses are summarized in Tab 5.1.

Surveys of working systems e.g. Buchanan (1986) reveal that in practice, most systems are used in an advisory role rather than a controlling role. Some authors go further, suggesting that because of the finite limits placed upon the knowledge available within a knowledge base, the human user will always retain the principal role:

WHO ?		
	Expert users	**Novice users**
H **O** **W** **?**	Decision Support Second Opinion First Estimate What If Simulation Training	Consultation Learning

Tab. 5.1 Uses of expert systems.

'But if human decision making really is based upon tree-like rules, then the number of rules needed is infinitely long - a reductio ad absurdum. This is not to say that rule-based expert systems cannot be highly successful, but only that they will need their human end-users to continue to supply the major part of the expertise.' (Collins,1987).

If Collins' view is accepted, then the total knowledge used by the system to tackle a problem becomes the machine-representable knowledge and the user's own knowledge.

5.1.2 The Tripartite System Model

If we are to consider a system which integrates expert systems with another information system, then we require a more sophisticated model of HCI than the traditional view of man and machine. The system may be represented in terms of a tripartite model: human user, computer as information processor, computer as knowledge processor.

Within such a system view, it is necessary to consider not just the traditional human-computer interaction, but three distinct interactions:

- human-knowledge based interaction,
- human-information based interaction and
- knowledge based-information based interaction

In the traditional system, illustrated in Fig. 5.4(a), division of labour tends to occur by default. The computer handles the task set, and the user generally carries out some analysis on the results. Consider, for example, the enhancement of images by digital image processing. The computer processes a digital image, producing an enhanced result, which is then analysed by the user. In the tripartite system model, illustrated in Fig. 5.4(b), the allocation of tasks in order to produce an optimal solution is more complex and requires careful analysis.

This will be considered in the next section.

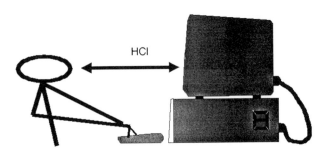

HCI = human/computer interaction

(a) Traditional view

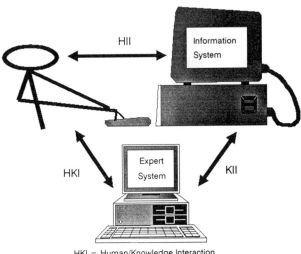

HKI = Human/Knowledge Interaction
HII = Human/Information Interaction
KII = Knowledge/Information Interaction

(b) Model for integrated system

Fig. 5.4 Models of human/computer interaction.

5.2 What humans and computers do well

The tripartite model of systems is based upon the view that each of the three agencies has their own blend of strengths and weaknesses, and by a careful analysis of these strengths and weaknesses, we may arrive at an optimum solution. The problem is analogous to that faced by a personnel manager in allocating tasks to a team of three subordinates. The assignment of tasks is based upon matching skills to requirements.(Fig. 5.5.)

Ms A is a great communicator, Mr B is a meticulous but unoriginal worker, and Dr C is an innovator, but gets bored easily. Faced with this problem on the basis of a knowledge of the strengths and weaknesses of each member of the team, a manager might allocate labour in the following way: Dr. C designs the product, Mr B builds it and Ms A sells it. The starting point of such an analysis must be an assessment of the strengths and weaknesses of each person or agency.

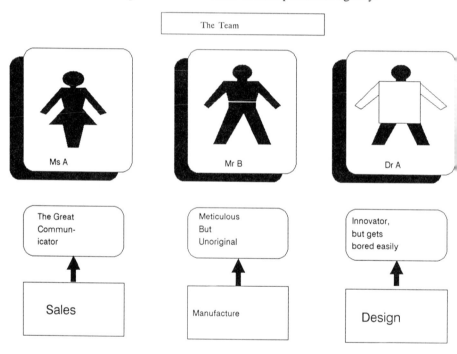

Fig. 5.5 Task allocation to human agents.

Consider first the user. Pew (1983) points to a number of areas where the user can outperform the computer:

'They have the ability to function very effectively as monitors. That is, they can be used to monitor the behaviour of a system, looking for abnormal situations as well as the normal progress of a system in operation.

They have the ability to locate and recognize patterns either in terms of display images or in terms of behaviour. They are also capable of doing several tasks in parallel.

They have great versatility in handling many different input and output symbols.

They have the ability to adapt to a situation that involves risk and uncertainty and can quickly guide a computer-based system where decisions have to be made quickly and intuitively on data that itself may be subject to error.'

At the same time, they show certain limitations when compared with computers:

- They are relatively slow information processors.
- They can show inconsistencies and errors.
- They may well lack specific expertise in some areas.
- They have fuzzy limits of expertise.

Conventional information systems may be described as effective but limited. They perform a limited set of operations upon a limited set of data types. Within this operating range, they do so efficiently, reliably and consistently.

Expert systems attempt to model human expertise. They, therefore, take on some of the human attributes. Inevitably, they also have human weaknesses and some of their own. The nature of knowledge available to an expert system is limited to that which can be represented on a machine. This is generally specific and detailed knowledge about a narrow problem domain. In many situations, the human being uses a wide range of experiential knowledge or common sense. In such situations it is difficult for an expert system to match human performance. The relative strengths of each agency are illustrated in Fig. 5.6:

5.2.1 Task allocation

The key to producing a successful system is now dependent upon allocating appropriate tasks to each agent and ensuring proper communication between the different agencies. The problem must first be divided up into tasks suitable for allocation. A reductionist strategy may be adopted, similar to that of some methodologies in conventional software engineering, for example, the Information Engineering Methodology (IEM) encapsulated in the CASE tool IEF, as described in the previous chapter.

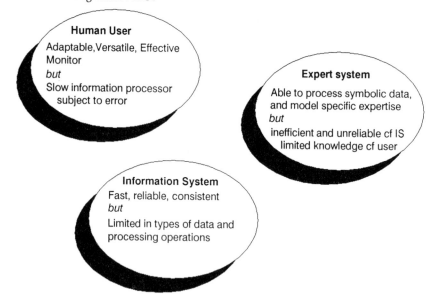

Fig. 5.6 Strengths and weaknesses.

Experience from expert systems has shown that this reductionist approach may not be easily accepted by experts, from whom a knowledge of the problem may be gleaned. This may due to very real problems in analysis, or due to a reluctance to dissect their own expertise. The use of tools in the analysis may help in this process.

In conventional knowledge engineering, this stage often forms a bottleneck. The demands made by task allocation are not as great as in conventional knowledge engineering, since it is necessary to break down each task to the elemental level which may be represented by rules or frames or other knowledge representation scheme. In this case, the initial analysis required only to elucidate a level of detail sufficient to identify individual tasks (Fig 5.7).

Once such a task analysis is carried out, it is necessary to assign the tasks to the most appropriate agency: human, machine as knowledge processor, and machine as information processor. At this stage, each task may be viewed as a module in a notional modular piece of software. The allocation of tasks is influenced by the strengths and weaknesses, summarized in Fig. 5.6.

The consequences for task allocation are as follows :

- The computer as information processor is best at representing any module which can be represented without resort to symbolic reasoning.
- The computer as knowledge processor is best suited to specific and narrowly defined problems. It must be kept within the bounds of its knowledge base.
- The human user is the most effective monitor, provided that specific expertise is not required beyond the capabilities of the user.

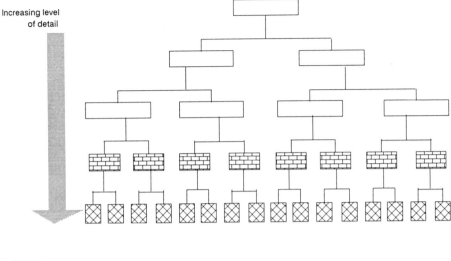

Increasing level
of detail

Level of detail required for task allocation (procedures)

Level of detail required for knowledge representation
rules, frames, etc.

Fig. 5.7 Detail required for task analysis.

Based upon these strengths and weaknesses, task allocation may proceed in accordance with the guidelines shown in Tab. 5.2. The process of the allocation of tasks is summarized in Fig 5.8.

Once each task is allocated, the corresponding module may be tackled using conventional methods. The information processing modules may be designed as conventional structured code, typically in a language such as C or Pascal. The design of the knowledge-based modules will depend upon the demands placed upon them. Many may also be designed in conventional third generation languages. If this proves inadequate, then a more flexible language specifically designed to handle AI problems, such as PROLOG may be employed. This will increase design complexity, requiring interfacing to conventional code. The system is built on modular lines, and as such should possess many of the software virtues traditionally associated with structured programs, e.g maintainability, testability, adaptability, reusability.

5.3 Interfaces for the tripartite system model

The design of the physical human-computer interface has been the subject of substantial research, and a recent account has been provided by Long and Dowell (1989). It has been pointed out that much of this research has been carried out by members of the social science community, and that interfaces have been neglected

Two broad trends may be noted, as we move from the computer as information processor through the computer as knowledge processor to the human user. The flexibility increases, as consistency and reliability decreases.

In allocating each module, the first choice should be the most reliable method. If this is not flexible enough, the next most reliable agency should be considered.

If none of them are adequate, a combination of agencies should be considered.

If a combination could be employed, then the task should be subdivided further into elemental tasks, which may be allocated to single agencies.

Tab. 5.2 Guidelines for task allocation.

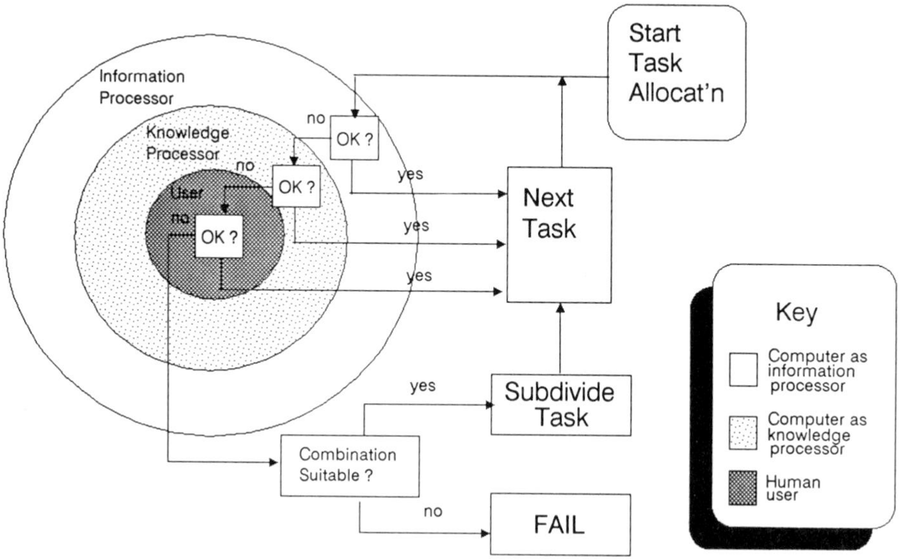

Fig. 5.8 The process of task allocation.

by the software engineers (Sommerville, 1989). If the user is to be considered as a part of the system from an early stage, this can no longer be the case. Associated with the tripartite system model, three types of interface are now required:

- The human-information processor interface
- The human-knowledge processor interface
- The information-knowledge processor interface

Fortunately, each of these areas has been the subject of substantial research in their own right, and we shall consider each in turn..

5.3.1 The human-information processor interface

The traditional study of human-computer interfaces forms the basis of the human-information processing interface. Such interfaces were initially command-driven, that is, instructions to the computer were presented as commands e.g. Copy a:myprog c:

Whilst such interfaces still find favour with experienced users, inexperienced do not intuitively make the leap from 'copy the file myprog from drive a: to drive c:' to ' Copy a:myprog c:'.. There is a learning curve associated with the user learning the required set of commands, or command language.

An alternative approach was sought to provide a more accessible interface, and the initial application was office automation systems. Much of the current work is strongly influenced by the work on the STAR interface, done at Rank Xerox Palo Alto labs, and leading to the WIMP (Windows, Icons, Menus, Pointer) systems currently in vogue. (Fig 5.9).

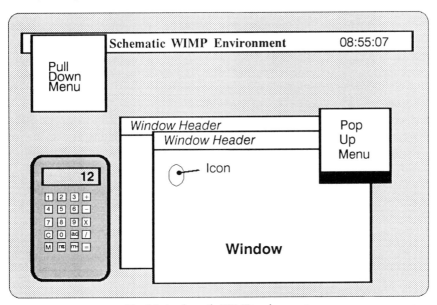

Fig. 5.9 A schematic WIMP environment.

A standard for developing WIMP environments, originated by MIT, is currently being promoted by a number of hardware manufacturers under the X Windows banner (Scheifler *et al*, 1986). However, a number of portability issues remain unresolved.

The WIMP philosophy is based upon attempts to provide an interface that mimics clerical operations, drawing on its origin in office automation systems. The philosophy is based upon three principal metaphorical representations:

The Concrete Object Metaphor. This seeks to base computer operations upon corresponding actions in 'real-life'. Thus, a file is erased by dragging it physically from its own directory to an icon representing a 'trash can'.

What You See Is What You Get (WYSIWYG) This seeks to present the user with a screen analogous to a piece of paper. Every action is immediately put up on the screen, presenting an immediate status message that an action has been carried out.

The DeskTop Metaphor. The interface screen is based upon a desk. At the user's disposal are a number of documents and a range of tools e.g. Calculator,Clock, Diary. Simultaneous and rapid access to any number of documents and tools should be provided, if the flexibility of an actual desktop is to matched.

The term 'direct manipulation' (DM) has been coined to describe this approach, since the windows and other data items in the system are manipulated directly rather than by means of command strings. Direct manipulation interfaces were developed specifically for inexperienced users and are certainly more accessible, reducing the learning time. However, they can act as a constraint for more experienced users, imposing a particular model of dialogue upon the user (Fig. 5.10).

The benefits and weaknesses of DM interfaces, compared to command-driven interfaces, are summarized in Tab. 5.3.

Perhaps the biggest barrier to the acceptance of such interfaces lies in their uneasy relationship with the ubiquitous PC. Although GEM is available for the PC, the implementation is limited in power and flexibility compared with other more powerful machines. As acceptance of the use of a mouse with the PC grows and more powerful processors are incorporated, this will become less of a problem.

5.3.2 The human-knowledge processor interface

The human-knowledge processor interface has been considered as the 'explanation' mechanism associated with classical expert systems. The field of explanation was surveyed by Berry and Broadbent (1986,1987), and the interested reader is pointed to their articles for a detailed survey.

Comparison of learning curves for two principal interface types

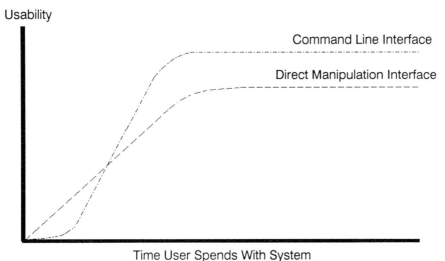

Fig. 5.10 Usability of interface types over time.

The explanation facilities associated with expert systems have been used in a number of ways:

(a) Description of Reasoning Path. The most basic facility is a 'trace-back' facility, citing the rules invoked to arrive at a conclusion.

(b) Testing. A competent explanation enables the system designer to examine whether the conclusions reached are reasonable. Since in a system of any complexity, it is not possible to test all possibilities, the implication is made that if the system works well for known cases, then provided its working limits are not breached, it will perform satisfactorily.

(c) Expert feedback. A competent explanation facility allows the original expert to check that their knowledge has been represented correctly.

(d) *User confidence.* The availability of explanation boosts the users confidence in the results.

(e) *Training.* Explanation can facilitate training by leading the user through the stages needed to arrive at a solution.

	Benefits	**Drawbacks**
Icons	Reminders Occupy small area Can be intuitive	May require text as well as pictoral representation Can be confusing
Multiple **Windows**	Allows simultaneous access to - more information - multiple sources - different perspectives - different levels - multitasking	Multiple access may not increase - absorption - comprehension
Direct **Manip-** **ulation**	Initially visuallyattractive Reduces learning curve Eliminates need for command language Consistency across applications WYSIWYG Undo facility	Can be slower in use than command driven interface for experienced user Makes heavy demands upon memory and processing power Wildcard facility more flexible than corresponding rubberbanding function Can act as constraint upon user dialogue Limited PC compatibility

Tab. 5.3 Benefits and drawbacks of DM interfaces.

In practice, the explanation facilities provided are often limited to a simple rule-tracing facility, and user response is mixed (see O'Neill and Morris, 1989). More sophisticated approaches have been suggested e.g. Swartout (1983), but generally, suffer from their own complexity. The effort required to provide truly effective explanation may well exceed that required to implement the rest of the system.

5.3.3 The information-knowledge processor interface

The study of interfaces between expert systems and other information systems has been dominated by the study of interfaces between expert systems and database management systems. This work is summarized in an article by Torsun and Ng (1989), and their work is cited in Case Study III in Chapter 9.

They divide systems into two types: tightly-coupled and loosely-coupled systems. In loosely-coupled systems, the two entities (E.S and DBMS) are kept entirely separate, with the expert system being invoked where required. The problem here is maintaining consistency if the database is being constantly updated. The advantage is the simplicity of the interface and the possibility to add on an E.S to an existing database system. A system of this type has been described by Jarke and Vassiliou (1984).

Tightly-coupled Interfaces	Loosely-coupled Interfaces
Requires closely-linked development of expert system and DBMS	Separate development of expert system and DBMS is possible
Not possible to add-on expert system to existing DBMS	Possible to add on expert system to existing DBMS
Complex Interface Design	Simpler Interface Design
Improves consistency and reduces maintenance costs	Problems with maintenance & consistency

Tab. 5.4 Comparison of coupling schemes.

The alternative tightly coupled approach, uses the database system as an extension of the internal database of the expert system by on-line communications channels. This requires a more sophisticated interface, but overcomes many of the problems of consistency. The two types of interface are compared in Tab. 5.4.

5.3.4 Integrating The Interfaces

In any integrated system, the problem facing the software engineer is how to integrate the information-based and knowledge-based components of the human-computer interface, since in such a system, they must be part of the same physical interface. One possible solution lies in the application of topic-based explanation, described by Southwick(1989).

He identifies a weakness of rule tracing in terms of discontinuities in the line of reasoning, with a consequent user dissatisfaction at the apparent illogicality of the line of questioning. This leads him to approach explanation by defining the current topic being explored, and keeping the user informed about it. A landmark is defined when a line of questioning changes from one topic to another. If the

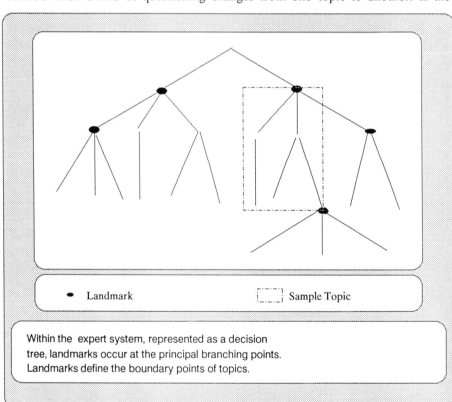

Within the expert system, represented as a decision
tree, landmarks occur at the principal branching points.
Landmarks define the boundary points of topics.

Fig. 5.11 Landmarks within an expert system.

system is envisaged in terms of a decision tree, then the landmarks occur at the principal branching points (Fig. 5.11).

This type of explanation is of interest for integrated systems since such a system is envisaged in modular form, providing natural landmarks for Southwick's system. Within each task module further landmarks are provided either by principal branching points in the decision tree within knowledge-based modules or by procedure boundaries within structured programming code for information processing. The availability of landmarks for both knowledge- and information-based modules provides the necessary integration between the human-knowledge-based component and the human-information based component.(Fig. 5.12)

Once the landmarks have been assigned, the presentation of topic information may be carried out using either a command-driven interface or a direct manipulation interface. As well as the strengths and weaknesses already discussed, the choice of interface will be affected by a number of additional factors:

(a) *The experience of the user.* Note that we are not considering the user's experience in the problem domain, but rather their level of expertise with computers themselves.

(b) *The type of information.* Most expert systems deal in textual representations of knowledge. Graphical information may well favour the direct manipulation approach.

(c) *House Style.* If the existing interfaces are all of one type in an organization, it is a strong incentive to retain a consistent 'house style'.

In his article, Southwick describes such a system for a supplementary benefit system (Fig. 5.13). The facility was command driven. An alternative based upon direct manipulation ideas is presented in Fig. 5.14.

The human-computer interface may be implemented in either the 3GL used elsewhere in the system, or if a graphical direct manipulation interface is required, using dedicated tools, where such tools are provided. The tools available will vary from machine to machine, from the graphics toolbox provided with PC 3GL compilers, to sophisticated tools such as SunTools and Sunview from Sun Microsystems. Many of these sophisticated tools are based upon the X Windows standard. Unfortunately, these higher level tools aimed at interface design make use of proprietary components which nullify the portability of the implemented interfaces.

An independently implemented interface brings advantages in terms of maintainability, adaptability, and portability. However, it can also perpetuate the myth that human issues are limited to the interface itself, and that as such consideration of such issues can be left to the postcoding phase.

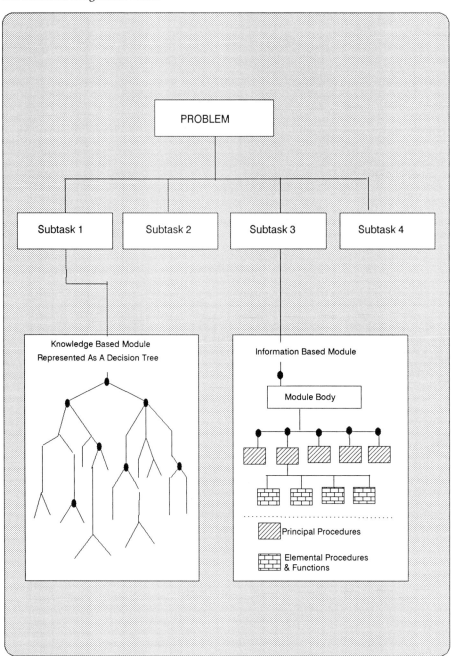

Fig. 5.12 Landmarks within an integrated system.

Current Topic : Mary is entitled to sup.benefit

There are two ways to solve this goal :
1. Mary entitled to supplementary pension
2. Mary entitled to supplementary allowance

Action : HELP

You can enter one of : 1 2 go fail succeed
why help stop
Action : 1

Description : We are now entering the body of the Supplementary Benefit
Act. There are two ways to show entitlement - by showing that the client is
entitled to a pension or to a supplementary allowance.

Topic Hierarchy

   Mary is entitled
   Mary has given basic details
   Mary is entitled to supplementary benefit

Fig. 5.13 Explanation screen (after Southwick).

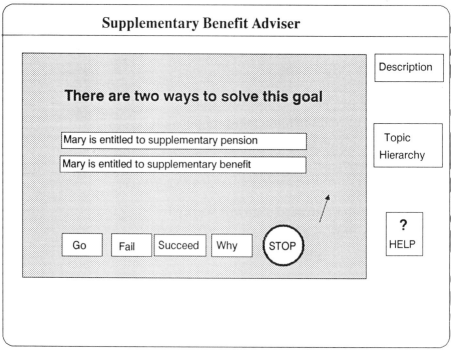

Fig. 5.14 Direct manipulation interface.

5.3.5 Intelligent Interfaces

Both command-driven and direct manipulation interfaces are classified as 'dumb' interfaces. An alternative approach is the so-called 'intelligent' interface. The goals of providing an 'intelligent' interface are to enhance the interface in a number of ways.

- increasing the number of input and output media
- enriching the input-output grammar
- attempting to co-operate with the user in the achievement of task goals
- the ability to adapt to different users

(Coats and Vlaeminke,1987)

Whilst active research is ongoing in this area, e.g. Tang *et al* (1989), Sleeman and Ward (1989), the current state of the art is insufficiently devloped to be of use to system designers. Current problems include the provision of reliable machine learning, comprehension of natural language and the provision of a world model to allow the interface to interpret inputs in context. Over the next few years, we are likely to see limited intelligence incorporated into commercial interfaces, whilst AI researchers will continue to inprove the performance of research prototypes.

5.4 Problem Solving by Tripartite Systems

In order to illustrate the ideas in this chapter, let us consider how they might be applied to two very different problems. The solving of crossword puzzles is a task requiring many of the cognitive skills that one might traditionally associate with human intelligence. A computer solution might be based upon two different approaches:

The classical AI solution: In this approach, a crossword solver would be approached by a knowledge engineer who would try to glean from the expert a working knowledge of how he tackles the problem, probably by structured interview. After this knowledge elicitation exercise, the knowledge engineer would seek to represent the knowledge of the expert in machine representable form, i.e. rules, frames or similar. Once this was achieved, the system could be implemented using either a shell or a specialist AI language such as LISP or PROLOG.

The traditional information processing approach. Using conventional information processing techniques, the modelling of the expert's approach may not be open to us. Instead, an efficient algorithm is required to carry out sorting and pattern matching techniques. Emphasis would be placed upon improving the efficiency of such an algorithm, so that each 'sort and match' operation occupies the minimum time.

Both approaches are problematic. The traditional AI route has often produced systems aimed at solving similar problems which although attractive on paper, are inefficient and unreliable in practical use. The traditional information processing route is likely to be overwhelmed by the sheer amount of processing required to solve a clue. A pragmatic approach might seek to combine the strengths of the AI solution with the reliability of the information processing approach, and incorporate the strengths of the user as well.

Consider the following approach. Crossword clues may be divided into 8 types defined in Tab. 5.5 .

The computer has the ability to search a large vocabulary rapidly and exhaustively. The human being has the ability to see tenuous or indirect connections. The computer performs pattern matching efficiently and is not misdirected by line ends, spaces, punctuation. However, some clues are a combination of types, and these are much more difficult for the computer. Of the 8 types of clues, at least 3 are amenable to direct computer solution: Hidden, Reversed, Anagrams.

The following clue is presented for solution: *'Cart in yard overturned' (4)*

The clue may be tested for solutions of the hidden, reversal and anagram types. Hidden and reversal solutions may be checked in similar ways. First, the clue is turned into a string of characters, devoid of punctuation and irrespective of case:

'cartinyardoverturned'

Double Meaning Two different definitions are given for the same word ,

e.g. 'Drum for a couple of cats' (3-3) = tom-tom

Pun The answer sounds like a different word,

e.g. 'Watch out ! a quartet of golfballs on its way' (4) = fore (four)

Hidden The answer is hidden in the words of the clue itself,

e.g. 'Proprietor skulking in shad<u>ow ner</u>vously' (5) = owner

e.g . ' Chea<u>t own</u>er of large village (4) = town

Reversal The answer becomes another word when reversed,

e.g. 'Cart in <u>yard</u> overturned' (4) = dray

e.g. ' Statue <u>sore</u> at being turned upside down' (4) = Eros

Anagram The answer is made up of letters of another word or words,

e.g. '<u>I lied</u>, tipsy with <u>rum</u> causing wild excitement' (8) = delirium

e.g. '<u>Hear</u> the voice of Zeus' wife' (4) = Hera

Charade The answer is split into two or more parts,

e.g. 'Capone has his methods - work every time' (6)

= 'Al' + 'ways' = Always

e.g. 'Rip marks out of carpet - signs of weeping !(10)

= 'tear' + 'stains' = 'tearstains'

Ins and Outs The answer will have one word inside another,

e.g. 'Males in TV commercial - makes a change ' (5)

= 'men' inside 'ad' = amend

e.g. 'A choice between good men' (4) = 'or' inside 'st.' = sort

Bits and Pieces The subsiduary part of the clue is a single letter, usually a direction (N,S,E,W) or similar,

e.g. 'Look after Granny on motor trip to the East' (4) = Care

Tab. 5.5 Types of crossword clues.

The computer then searches for strings of the required length against a lexicon, to suggest hidden words:

cart arti rtin tiny inya nyar yard ardo rdov dove over vert ertu rtur turn urne rned

From which the computer is likely to match the following groups with the lexicon:

cart tiny yard dove over turn

From these 'yard' and 'cart' can be eliminated because they are present in the original clue. Thus, the computer will suggest 'tiny', 'dove', 'over' and 'turn'. If there are any letters known these may be used as a further sieve.

In order to find any reversed words, the string used above is simply inverted i.e. *'cartinyardoverturned'* becomes *'denrutrevodraynitrac'*

After this the process is similar to analysis for hidden solutions. The computer first scans for word groups from which the computer will select 'dray'. Once again, this may be checked against any known letters.

When we consider anagrams, the inadequacy of the matching approach is revealed. In looking for anagrams, a simple pattern matching mechanism is insufficient. If we consider the same clue, a relatively simple one there are 20 letters to choose from. The number of 4 letter combinations to check is 20P4 or 116,280. (The notation nPm refers to the number of ways to select n objects from a total of m).

A more complex case might involve 8 letters from 30, 30P8 or 2.36×10^{11}! Fortunately, we have knowledge about conventions used in anagrams. Only complete words or generally considered, so that we can eliminate much sorting.

We can use the following knowledge to restrict the sort:

- Any anagram involves 4 letters
- These 4 letters must come from a complete word or set of words.
- The words themselves can be ignored, and their reverses have already been considered.

This cuts down the sort to 'cart' and 'yard', 2 x 4P4 = 48 combinations, and of these 4 may be ignored: 'cart', 'trac', 'yard' and 'dray', leaving just 44 to check:

catr crat crta ctra ctar acrt actr arct artc atrc atcr
tarc tacr tcar tcra trca rcat rcta rtca rtac ract ratc
yadr yrad yrda ydra ydar ayrd aydr adyr adry ardy aryd
ryad ryda rday rdya rady rayd drya dyar dyra dayr dary

None of which are likely to produce a match with the lexicon. The possibility of finding an anagram is eliminated after just 44 matching operations, as against over 100,000.

The example anagram clue 'I lied, tipsy with rum, causing wild excitement' (8) illustrates the need to check all combinations of words adding up to the correct length, as the solution 'delirium' is derived from three word groups, 'I-rum-lied'. Whilst this is more complex than the last example (8 x 8P8 = 8 x 8! = 322,560

ACROSS

1. To stammer tripe at a gallop ! (4)
4. I lied, tipsy with rum, causing wild excitement (8)
6. Watch out - a quartet of golfballs on its way (4)
7. A choice between good men (4)
12. as 11 (4)
13. Statue sore at being turned upside down (4)
14. Rip marks out of carpet - signs of weeping ! (10)

DOWN

1. Look after Granny on motor trip to the East (4)
2. Drum for a couple of cats (3-3)
3. Capone has his methods - work every time (6)
4. Cart in yard overturned (4)
5. Males in TV commercial - makes a change (5)
8 Proprietor skulking in shadow, nervously (5)
9. as 6 (4)
10. Hear the voice of Zeus' wife (4)
11. Cheat owner of large village (4)

Fig. 5.15 Example clues arranged in a crossword.

Clue :   'Cart in yard overturned (4)

Current Topic : Anagrams

Input Clue :   'Cart in yard overturned
Length   :   4

Checking for hidden words.....
Checking for reversed words....
Checking for anagrams...

Possible Solutions

    tiny   dove   over   turn
    dray

Explanations
....t in y....   Hidden   yard Reversed = dray
.....d   ove....   Hidden
    over......   Hidden
......turn......   Hidden   No Anagrams reported

Fig. 5.16 Explananation screen for a support system.

possible combinations), it is clearly less than the blind sort on 38P8 (*ca.* 200 million million combinations).

A computer solution could, therefore, take the form of a decision support system, conforming to Collins' view of the human retaining overall control. The human role of monitor is retained. In practice, a decision support system for crossword solvers would include other facilities such as a Thesaurus. By retaining the human control, the computer may be left to do what it does best, process information. The use of knowledge encapsulated within those computer operations can bring substantial benefits. Explanation in such a system could be based upon the topic-based scheme. A typical screen is shown in Fig 5.16

Whilst this may seem like a 'toy' domain, the point is made that by the incorporation of rules into a relatively conventional sorting routine, the numbers of operations required may be reduced dramatically. This point is backed up by a look at the literature, where the integration of expert systems with conventional information systems occurs most frequently in the area of database management systems, where expert systems can clearly reduce processing overheads.

As a contrast to this tricky but toy problem consider the information requirements of a newsagents' shop.

His principal business is the sale of newspapers and magazines. These are complicated by the provision of a delivery service. In addition, he carries a limited stock of stationery items, cards and sweets. He has a small workforce, but they each work different part-time hours, and at different rates of pay, according to their age. Some are included in National Insurance and PAYE. Some work sufficient hours to gain legal entitlement to statutory sick pay and paid holiday.

His business functions may be divided into four categories, stock control, newspapers, payroll and customer service. In providing a computer system to support these applications, each function should be considered in turn:

Stock Control. The range of items required as stock by the newsagent is relatively large. His great advantage is the convenience to the customer of picking up odd items at the corner. However, without careful stock control, he may end up with much capital tied in useless stock.

Newspapers. Most people come into the shop primarily for their newspapers. This may lead to secondary purchases, which may prove more profitable than the initial sale, but that initial sale is essential to attract the customer. People are very fussy about newspapers, and a good newsagent may well have a knowledge of which papers are an acceptable substitute if the customer's first choice is missing. The delivery system requires administration, and bills need to be collected.

Payroll. Although his staff will be small, each member of that staff may require different working conditions, due to age and hours worked. The rules governing NI contributions from part-time workers and hours worked by young people are relatively complicated.

Customer Service. The bottom line in any shop is the service provided to the customer. This will depend upon other functions such as stock control, as well as the encounter with staff.

In considering a computer system to support these functions, we may divide up the required functionality into the four principal functions. Each function may be then considered for the best agent for the job: information processor, knowledge processor and human user.

Consider stock control. The function may be considered in three separate stages: recording stock levels, keeping stock records and predicting reordering requirements. Traditionally, the stock level would be recorded by a shop assistant in a stock ledger, which provides the stock records. On the basis of this a senior assistant or the proprietor can make judgements about the reordering level required. In providing a computer system we can reduce data entry errors at the first stage, and if we automate the reordering, we may free the proprietor for other duties.

Stock control may be achieved by bar code reading at the point of sale. Record keeping can be achieved by use of a DBMS which can provide any required data in the form of reports. The use of the computer as information processor is inadequate at the final stage, where use of an expert system would permit automatic reordering when stock reached a particular level. The expert system would take as input the data from the database within the DBMS. The system could be written either in terms of general rules, such as

IF stock level of HB pencils   average of last four weeks sales THEN
  Reorder 2 x (average of last four weeks sales)

or in the form of specific rules to take account of seasonal factors e.g

IF start of school term **THEN**
  Reorder 4 x (average of last four weeks sales (HB pencils))
IF November **THEN** Reorder Christmas Cards

In practice, it would be difficult to cover all such seasonal eventualities, especially within the constraints of a practical system. It would, therefore, be necessary to incorporate a human monitoring process to check the results of the expert system, and to ensure that account was taken of abnormal factors e.g a heat wave in the summer producing an extra demand for ice cream.

In such a combination, the best possible solution could be achieved, whilst the proprietor could ensure that icecream was available in a heat wave, the expert system would ensure that they did not run out of routine items such as rubber bands.

Newspaper orders present a somewhat different problem. The information problem is about keeping track of a routine but complicated operation. The process is about managing information rather than making a judgement. Where a judgement is required, it may be satisfied by a simple piece of information such as which papers form an acceptable substitute for the regular order. This may be achieved by a conventional DBMS. The database records might look like Fig. 5.17.

The problem of keeping track of staff is complicated by the variety of staff and the variety of regulations concerning them. The problem is, however, well defined and is unlikely to produce anomalies. The details of each member of staff can be handled readily by a DBMS, with details kept of staff age, starting date, hours worked per week and so on. However, the job of translating this data into a weekly wage and handling other related matters is better left to an expert system. Such a system would take as input the routine data, alongside any anomalous events, particularly overtime worked. The knowledge base would include rules linking rates of pay to age, rules concerning statutory deduction such as PAYE, NI contributions. Such a system would invariably include a large component of numerical reasoning. e.g

IF weekly_wage   (personal tax allowance/52) **THEN**
  PAYE deduction: = 0
ELSE
  PAYE deduction: = weekly_wage - (personal tax allowance/52) * 0.25

It could also warn the proprietor about breaches of regulations concerning number of hours to be worked by juveniles:

IF age < 16 **AND** hours_worked legal_maximum_for_juveniles **THEN**
  GENERATE_REPORT (WARNING! Legal Limit on hours exceeded)

Finally, counter service is best left to the human. The computer can optimize levels of stock for profitability and availability, it can ensure that the proprietor knows which is the customer's favourite newspaper, but in any task, there is nearly always something the human does best! The overall information system is illustrated in Fig. 5.18.

In the case studies, we shall see more details of solutions to real-world problems.

Customer Record No : 257

Customer Name	**Mr John Smith**
Customer Address	**6, High St., Lowton**

Daily Newspaper	**THE GUARDIAN**
Delivered By	**AJC**
Acceptable Substitute	**None**

Sunday Newspaper	**THE OBSERVER**
Delivered By	**BKD**
Acceptable Substitute	**THE CORRESPONDENT**

Other Order	**Radio times/TV Times**
Delivered On	**Thursday**

Weekly Charge	**£4.00**
Last Paid	**25.12.92**

Amount Outstanding	**£16.00**

Fig. 5.17 Database screen for newspaper orders.

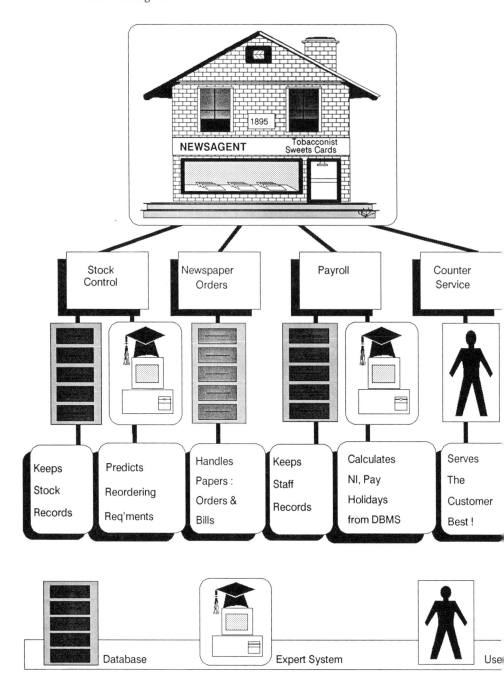

Fig. 5.18 Overall integrated solution for newsagent.

5.5 Further Reading

Two papers providing a good insight into the problems of providing interfaces for expert systems.
Although a few years old now, recent studies (Morris and O'Neill, 1989) confirm the continuing relevance of this work:
Berry, D. C. and Broadbent, D. E. (1986,1987) *Expert systems and the man-machine interface, Exp.Sys.* **3**(4) and **4**(1).

A realistic assessment of the capabilities of expert systems, together with a good case for the retention of human control in such systems:
Collins, H. M. (1987) Expert systems, Artificial Intelligence and the Behavioural Co-ordinates of Skill in *The Question of Artificial Intelligence: Philosophical and Sociological Perspectives*, (ed. B. Bloomfield), Croom-Helm.

The most recent survey of UK expert system activity at the time of writing. Despite the title, deals with most aspects of expert system design:
O'Neill, M. and Morris, A. (1989) Expert Systems in the United Kingdom: an evaluation of development methodologies, *Exp.Sys*, **6**(2) 90-9.

A good attempt to provide 'real' explanation facilities. Includes a good discussion of the issues involved:
Swartout, W. R. (1983) XPLAIN: a System for Creating and Explaining Expert Consulting Programs, *Art.Intell.*, **21**, 285-325.

CHAPTER SIX

Issues in integration: the assessment of quality

Quality assessment is a headache for all information systems. Much work has been done in the information systems area, though there is still more to do. Ideas from mainstream software development are not always suitable for expert systems or systems incorporating knowledge-based modules. In particular, models based upon sequential development methodologies, assuming a rigid specification are unsuitable. New metrics are required, and a reassessment must be made of the underlying characteristics of quality which are being represented.

In this chapter, we shall compare existing quality models, and examine their suitability for systems with expert system components. We shall examine the inter-relationships between different facets of quality, and present a model of quality in terms of both characteristics and their inter-relationships. We shall suggest approaches to how this model may be used to measure quality.

6.1 What is software quality?

Evaluating expert systems has in the past often been concerned with comparing the capabilities of different expert system development tools, particularly shells. As expert systems come out of the AI closet, the question of the quality of the systems themselves will become more important. Traditional software virtues such as reliability, maintainability and efficiency will be expected. There is a need for reassessing existing models of software quality to take account of the special needs of expert systems. Let's start with the basic question 'What is quality?'

6.1.1 What is quality?

Quality is one of those things that we can all recognise, but is hard to quantify. We may take as an example the purchase of a car. Some of the factors which may be considered to contribute to its quality, are shown in Fig. 6.1. The factors shown all contribute in some way to our view of quality. A number of features of quality may be deduced from this simple example.

(a) Quality is multi-faceted. It is not represented by any single parameter, but rather by a set of characteristics.

(b) Quality is not absolute, but relative. When we measure quality, there are no absolute benchmarks like the wavelength of light, against which we measure

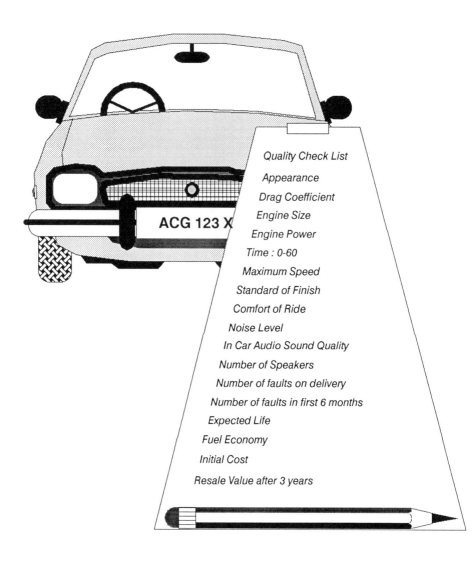

Fig. 6.1 Criteria of quality when buying a car.

length, or the time period of an oscillation of a crystal, against which we measure time.

(c) *Quality is subject to constraints.* Most people buying cars are constrained primarily by cost, which causes them to compromise on some aspects of quality.

(d) *Some aspects of quality can be measured* e.g. maximum speed, fuel economy. Often the most easily measured criteria are not the most important e.g. on the basis of fuel economy (which is a measure of 'greenhouse effect' atmospheric pollution through carbon dioxide emissions) and running costs, a 2CV outperforms most cars on the road, yet it is not stereotypical of a 'quality' car.

Many of these observations are also true of software quality. In the light of them, it is interesting to consider formal definitions of quality. The International Standards Organization (ISO) define quality as

'The totality of features and characteristics of a product or service that bear on its ability to satisfy stated or implied needs'

ISO (1986)

Different people have different needs and this can lead to various and conflicting views of quality.

6.1.2 Views of quality

Quality is a multidimensional quantity. Some of the principal dimensions might be considered as cost, timeliness, reliability, correctness, functionality and maintainability. A model of quality must reflect its multidimensional nature and we may use a visual analogy (Fig. 6.2). This visual analogy may be continued in order to consider different 'views' or perspectives (Fig. 6.3). Any single view tends to give us only a partial picture. The different views available have been classified in a number of ways e.g. user vs designer, client vs supplier. Such classifications tend to be stereotypical, but may be useful if understood in these terms.

Garvin (1984) has suggested five different views of quality:

1. *The transcendent view*: relates quality to innate excellence. Another word for this might be 'elegance'.
2. *The product-based view*: the economist's view - the higher the quality, the higher the cost.
3 *The user-based view* can be summarized as fitness for purpose. This will be defined later in the book as 'match-to-needs'.
4. *The manufacturing view*: quality measured in terms of conformance to requirements. As the requirements are laid down in a specification, this is referred to in this book as 'match-to-spec' quality'.

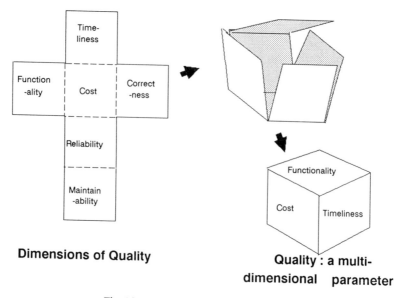

Dimensions of Quality

Quality : a multi-dimensional parameter

Fig. 6.2 Quality is a multidimensional construct

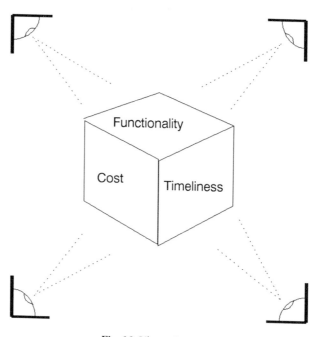

Fig. 6.3 Views of quality.

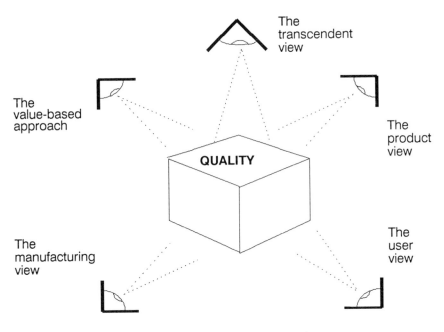

Fig. 6.4 Quality (after Garvin, 1984).

5. *The value-based view*: the ability to provide what the user wants at an affordable cost.

The Garvin views of quality are summarized in Fig. 6.4.

Another classification which is useful in the context of information systems is the distinction between manufacturing and design quality. Manufacturing quality is concerned with production of artefacts that fall within a specified range of tolerances for a set of defined criteria. It is usual in manufacturing for these criteria to be readily quantified. Design quality is much more subjective in nature than manufacturing quality. Design quality criteria are much less easy to quantify than manufacturing criteria. A good piece of design might be described as an elegant solution. How do you quantify elegance? The London Underground map has been heralded as a classic piece of 20th century design. This is a good piece of design because it fulfills the task required of it i.e. to provide the user with navigational information in a comprehensible format. It is an 'elegant' solution, but it is difficult to reflect 'elegance' in quantifiable ways. Our quality checklist (Fig. 6.1) contains both manufacturing and design criteria of quality.

Yasuda (1989) has recognized the need for both design and manufacturing quality in software. He identifies the fact that quality must ultimately be measured in terms of whether the person paying the bill is satisfied:

'Quality means the degree of user satisfaction. Previously, good quality meant that a national or an in-house standard was satisfied. This is necessary, but it is not sufficient alone for producing high quality products. Quality depends upon user satisfaction.'

He goes on to define two conditions necessary for quality:

- Software match to specification
- Specification match to user needs.

I shall refer to the first condition as 'match-to-spec' and the second as 'match-to-needs'. Too often, the emphasis within system development is on the match-to-spec to the point where the match-to-needs component is ignored, resulting in a product which the developer believes to be high quality, but does not produce customer satisfaction, because it does not address the user's needs. Match-to-spec quality is the software analogue of manufacturing quality. Match-to-needs quality covers the design aspects of quality.

Any model of quality must reflect the multidimensional nature of software quality, and takes account of both manufacturing and design aspects. It must also cope with the specific needs of expert systems. Let's start with a look at the existing models available.

6.2 Measuring information systems quality

One of the principal types of quality model employed is the hierarchical model of quality. This is illustrated schematically in Fig. 6.5. Models of this type represent quality as a set of criteria. Each criteria is then assessed by means of a metric. Two models are prevalent in the literature, due to McCall *et al* (1977) and Boehm *et al* (1978). A more recent study by Watts (1987) is based heavily upon McCall's original work.

The MQ model of Watts attempts to describe software quality in terms of a broad range of characteristics concerned with product operation, product revision and product transition. They are summarized in Tab. 6.1.

Some of the definitions provided here have been changed from the originals to provide a positive statement, e.g. maintainability is generally measured as the effort required to fix an error, but the criteria itself refers to the ease of fixing errors.

Without consideration of the additional assessment problems associated with expert systems, the MQ model suffers from four principal limitations:

- The emphasis on technical issues reflecting a designer's view
- The lack of satisfactory metrics
- The lack of a overall quality view
- A failure to represent the inter-relationships between criteria and metrics.

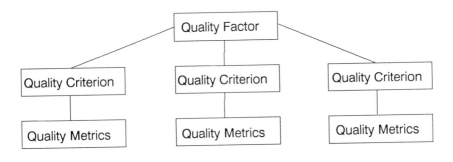

Fig. 6.5 The hierarchical view of quality.

Usability is concerned with the ease of use of the software.

Security is concerned with the protection of the program from unauthorized access.

Efficiency falls into two categories: execution efficiency and storage efficiency, both concerned with use of resources.

Correctness is the extent to which a program fulfills its specification.

Reliability is the ability of the system to perform without failure.

Maintainability is the ease of location and fixing of a fault.

Adaptability is the ease of making changes to the program.

Portability is the ease with which the system may be transferred from one environment to another.

Reusability is the extent to which the software may be reused in another context.

Interoperability is the ease with which the system may be coupled to another.

Tab. 6.1 The criteria associated with the MQ model.

6.2.1 The emphasis on technical quality criteria

The MQ model (and the other principal hierarchical models due to McCall and Boehm) consist of a set of criteria designed to measured the match to specification aspects of quality, those important to designers. There is little attempt to tackle 'fitness for purpose' quality. This is problematical when dealing with information systems, but disastrous when we consider expert systems. The reasons for this will be discussed below in section 6.3.

6.2.2 The problems with metrics

Watts (1987) suggests seven criteria of 'goodness' for a software metric.

1. *Objectivity.* The results should be from subjective influences. It must not matter who the measurer is.
2. *Reliability. The results should be stable, precise and repeatable.*
3. *Validity.* The metric must measure the correct characteristic.
4. *Standardization.* The metric must be unambiguous and allow for comparison.
5. *Comparability.* It must be comparable with other measures of the same criterion.
6. *Economy.* The simpler and, therefore, cheaper the measure is to use, the better.
7. *Usefulness.* The measure must address a need, not simply measure a property for its own sake.

A further important feature is *consistency*. Some measures appear to combine quite different factors. A measure should not be based upon a combination of apples and oranges, i.e., it should be dimensionally consistent.

Automation is also desirable. A measure that lends itself to convenient automation is clearly at an advantage. Such a measure is, by definition, objective, and automation boosts both economy and convenience.

Unfortunately, most of the metrics cited within the NCC study fail to meet the criteria laid down. They are often limited particularly in the areas of objectivity and validity. Where validity is suspected, it is often difficult to prove. In practice a major problem occurs because many metrics are based upon only a few fundamental measurable properties such as structuredness, readability and complexity. This has the effect that the metrics may relate to more than one quality criteria. This may or may not cause problems, but a one-to-one relationship between criteria and metrics is surely desirable.

6.2.3 The lack of an overall view of quality

The individual measures of software quality provided thus far do not provide an overall measure of software quality. For this, the individual measures must be combined. The individual measures of quality may conflict with each other, and compromises may have to be reached. The solution sought is an optimum balance of factors rather than an ideal solution. Perry (1983) has suggested that the inter-relationships may be represented in terms of direct, neutral or inverse relationships.

Some of the principal relationships between the criteria from the MQ model are described in Tab. 6.2. Perry's analysis, although very helpful, suffers from two drawbacks. The first is the assumption that the relationships are reversible. The author's work has shown that this is not always the case. Secondly, the relationships can be obscured by their application dependency. These limitations are addressed in the proposed quality model at the end of the chapter.

The second problem highlighted by the lack of an overall view of quality is the simplistic nature of many proposed schemes for combining metric scores by reduction to a single 'figure-of-merit'. Five such methods have been suggested for use with hierarchical models.

1. *Simple scoring.* In simple scoring, each criteria is allocated a score. The overall quality is given by the arithmetic mean of the individual scores.
2. *Weighted scoring.* This scheme allows the user to weight each criteria according to how important they consider them to be.
3. *Phased Weighting Factor Method.* This is an extension of weighted scoring. In this method, a weighting is assigned to a group of characteristics before each individual weighting is considered. Within the MQ model, the groupings might be based around the classification of product operation, product transition and product revision.
4. *The Kepner-Tregoe Method (1981).* In this method the criteria are divided into 'essential' and 'desirable'. A minimum value is specified for each essential criterion. Any software failing to reach these scores is designated unsuitable. 'Suitable' software is then judged by use of the weighting factor method.
5. *The Cologne Combination Method (Schmitz et al, 1975).* This method is designed with comparative evaluation in mind. Using the chosen criteria, each product is ranked in order.

Greater details of all these approaches are given in Watts (1987).

All these schemes are aimed at reducing the quality measure to a single parameter. An alternative approach, favoured by the author, retains the multi-dimensionality of quality, using polarity profiling. In this scheme quality is represented by a series of ranges from -3 to +3. The required quality may be represented, and compares to the actual quality. An example profile is given in Fig. 6.6.

In the example shown, the software is lacking in quality in the areas of efficiency and reliability. It is also worth noting that it is overengineered in terms of maintainability and adaptability. Much more information is available than from a single 'figure-of-merit'. This use of profiles to represent quality is developed later.

Integrity vs. Efficiency (inverse)

The control of access to data or software requires additional code and processing leading to a longer runtime and additional storage requirements.

Usability vs. Efficiency (inverse)

Improvements to the human-computer interface will require additional code and processing leading to a longer runtime and additional storage requirements.

Maintainability and Testability vs. Efficiency (inverse)

Optimized and compact code is not easy to maintain. Inevitably, well-structured well-commented and modular code is less efficient. This well-structured code is also easier to test.

Portability vs. Efficiency (inverse)

The use of optimized software or system utilities will lead to a reduction in portability.

Adaptability and Reusability vs. Integrity (inverse)

The general and flexible data structures required for flexible and reusable software increase the data security and integrity problems.

Reliability vs. Efficiency (neutral)

There is no reason why more reliable code should be either more or less efficient than less reliable code.

Maintainability vs. Adaptability and Reusability (direct)

Maintainable code is well-structured and easy to modify, making it easier to adapt and to re-use.

Tab. 6.2 Quality interrelationships (after Perry)

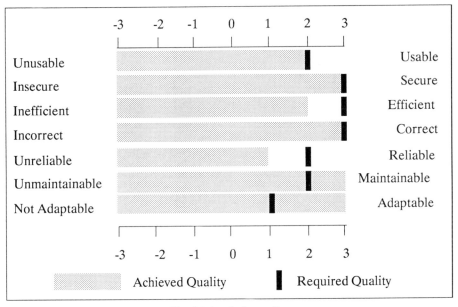

Fig. 6.6 A polarity profile.

6.2.4 The failure to represent the inter-relationships between criteria and metrics

The schematic hierarchical model, shown in Fig. 6.5, and often cited, is like any model, a simplification. The degree of simplification, however, is large, and misses a number of important features. Two of the most significant simplifications are that

- the criteria are not independent, and
- the relationships between criteria and metrics are many-to-many, not one-to-many.

Before considering a model of quality which seeks to address some of the limitations highlighted thus far, let us consider the specific quality needs of expert systems, both as stand-alone systems and integrated systems. In order to do this we must consider the specific problems of quality measurement associated with expert systems.

6.3 The specific problems relating to expert systems

Expert systems are different. This is the first commandment laid down in stone by the AI community and never to be broken by a true believer. At the risk of blaspheming, it is worth considering what makes expert systems difficult to assess.

Expert systems are complex. True. Any system that attains genuinely expert performance is likely to be complex. However, there are many complex systems in place around the world which at least, in theory, have been tested and constructed according under total quality management (TQM) systems. For example, all mission-critical systems supplied to the US Department of Defense (DoD) are supposed to have been developed according to the procedures of DoD 2167A.

Whilst it may be argued that existing TQM systems are not suitable for expert systems, it is unreasonable to argue that expert systems are qualitatively more complex than all other information systems.

Expert systems are dependent upon the expertise of a domain expert. Within knowledge engineering, the person who provides the knowledge is regarded as an 'expert'. In software engineering, it is generally assumed that the knowledge of the user can be readily modelled by the analyst. As a consequence, the role of the user is devalued. In many cases, this results in poor 'match-to-needs' quality. The necessary involvement of outside personnel in the development of expert systems should serve to highlight 'match-to-needs' aspects of quality. Whilst this will ultimately benefit the project, it may cause difficulties at the assessment stage, since these aspects are more difficult to measure than technical criteria.

Expert systems are designed by evolutionary methodologies rather than rigid waterfall lifecycle models. Also true, and many of the CASE tools, methodologies and TQM systems are tied to inappropriately rigid development models. However, the evolutionary approach proposed by Gilb (1988) provides a very effective evolutionary development technique, together with methods for the assessment of the quality of such systems.

Expert systems are targeted at ill-specified problems and 'match-to-spec' quality cannot be assessed. It is already been suggested that existing metrics for the assessment of information systems are inadequate. New methods of measurement are needed for all types of system. Such measures have been suggested by Gilb *(ibid)* for information systems designed by the evolutionary process. In the model proposed below for stand-alone and integrated expert systems, this concept is extended to cover such systems.

Much of the resistance to the introduction of CASE tools, and especially TQM systems in information systems comes from programmers and developers who fear their job being de-skilled and their creativity stifled. The proponents of such techniques tell us they that such fears are groundless. Whether this is true or not, the step from the basic principles of structured programming which have been accepted wisdom for a number of years is comparatively small. The corresponding step for expert system designers is much greater. It is, therefore, unsurprising that many expert system designers resist attempts to move towards a more disciplined and methodical approach to both design and quality management of expert systems design.

However, given current moves towards standards for TQM systems e.g. the increasing acceptance of ISO 9001 (BS5750 in the UK), this resistance provides one of the biggest stumbling blocks to the integration of expert systems into the mainstream information systems arena.

6.4 A scheme for expert system quality measurement

The approach to quality proposed in this section is built upon the foundations of the hierarchical models of Watts, McCall and Boehm. It also uses the idea of quality inter-relationships first suggested by Perry and makes use of profiling techniques. It is suggested with the particular needs of expert systems, stand-alone and integrated, in mind, but may also be used to assess conventional information systems.

The model consists of four components within an overall framework, shown in Fig. 6.7:

- A set of criteria.
- A set of inter-relationships.
- A set of measures, or performance indicators.
- A profiling scheme.

The first departure from existing approaches is the extra level of the hierarchy which views all criteria as a subset of correctness, and provides for the division into functional and business correctness. This requires the incorporation of new criteria associated with business correctness. This duality allows the model to reflect both user and designer views of quality. A specification drawn up along these lines would contain requirements, not just for the technical parameters, but also the business parameters. This in an attempt to improve 'match-to-needs' quality by bringing it into the specification. Each type of correctness is represented by quality criteria e.g. reliability, timeliness. Each criterion has performance targets associated with it, for measurement purposes.

The model is intended to address some of the limitations shown by other approaches. Some of the specific features of the model are listed below.

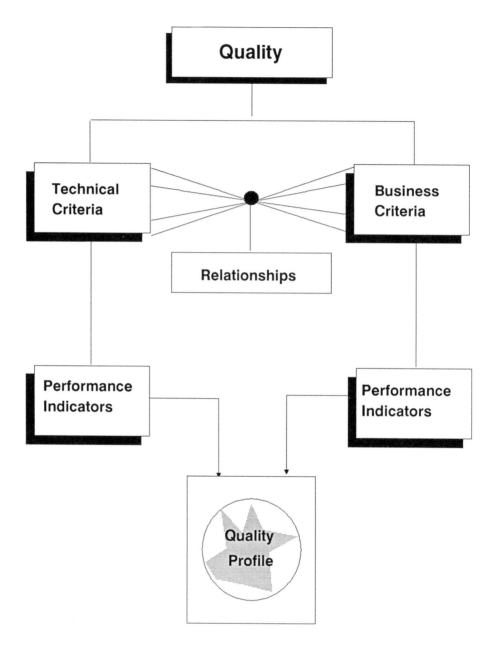

Fig. 6.7 Structure of new model.

Quality is considered in terms of

Technical correctness, which is the extent to which a system satisfies its functional specification,

and

Business correctness, which is the extent to which a system supports its departmental and strategic business objectives.

The following criteria are deemed to contribute to technical correctness :

Usability is the ease of use of the software.

Security is the extent to which unauthorized access to the program is prevented.

Efficiency is the relative amount of critical resources required to perform a function.

Reliability is the ability of the system to reproduce its function over a period of time without failure.

Maintainability is the ease of location and fixing of a fault.

Adaptability is the ease of making changes to the program.

Portability is the ease with which the system may be transferred from one environment to another.

The following criteria are considered to contribute to business correctness :

Timeliness is the extent to which delivery fits with the business deadlines and practices of the user.

Cost/Benefit is the extent to which the system satifies its cost/benefit expectations.

Ease of transition is the ease and effectiveness of assimilating information from existing systems.

Userfriendliness is the extent to which a system helps an operator carry out their job.

Tab. 6.3 Quality criteria.

(a) It is intended to be treated as a cohesive whole, but it is suggested that it may be adapted to the needs of a particular environment. The requirement is that the adaptations must be reflected throughout the model.

(b) It covers both business and technical criteria of quality, unlike previous hierarchical models, aiming to satisfy both the designer and user camps.

(c) It does not assume that the interrelationships are commutative, like Perry's work.

(d) It does not provide objective, comparable measures but does provide realizable and useful data about the quality of the system. Further, these measures are applicable to expert systems.

(e) The model is based upon the experience of practitioners gathered and collated by the author.

(f) The model makes use of performance indicators rather than traditional metrics, lending itself to the assessment of expert systems, stand-alone or integrated. It is also not tied to a sequential methodology, a useful feature for the assessment of expert systems.

A number of organizations were approached, each representing a different commercial sector: a software house, management consultants, a retail organization, a financial institution, a utility company and a manufacturing company. A knowledge elicitation exercise was carried out to elicit a set of quality criteria that reflected their needs. The starting point for all the discussions was the set of criteria associated with the MQ model.

The criteria used in this model, defined in Tab. 6.3, are drawn from the results of the six exercises. After a consensus had been reached with the participants as to an appropriate set of criteria, the relationships between them were explored using a grid and defining the relationships initially in terms of Perry's three types. However, in performing an overall analysis, the relationships between the criteria were found to be too complex and case-dependent to be represented by Perry's simple scheme of direct neutral and inverse. An alternative scheme is proposed by the author (Tab. 6.4), which indicates both the predominant type of relationship and the perceived strength of that relationship. The sign indicates the relationship type, the colour the strength of the relationship.

Using this scheme, the relationships are shown in Tab. 6.5. They are an important guide during development, indicating to the developer the likely impact of decisions to improve single aspects of quality.

However, once a system is developed, it is necessary to assess its performance. This is particularly important in the case of prototyping methodologies, where one

➕ Practically always Direct

➕ Direct in majority of cases

◎ No consistent relationship

▬ Inverse in a majority of cases

▬ Inverse in practically all cases

Tab. 6.4 Classification scheme for relationships.

is faced with the question, 'Is it good enough yet?'. One of the distinctive features of the model is the approach taken to measurement.

6.4.1 Measures for the quality model

The measures incorporated in this model are not 'metrics' in the traditional sense. They are not objective or transferable, but they do relate specifically to one criterion. They are designed such that they provide convenient ways of measuring the quality of systems in place. They aim to reflect the user's concerns about quality. They are also designed to provide data for a Quality Management System, should the organization put one into operation. Wherever possible they are cited as dimensionless percentages.

When assessing a human employee, the manager will set a series of 'performance targets'. These targets may well be linked to a performance-related pay scheme. As we attempt to model human expertise with computer systems, so it seems reasonable to think of setting the computer 'performance targets' and measuring the quality of the system accordingly. Going back to the pioneering days of MYCIN (Shortliffe, 1976), we could measure the quality of the system by a series of performance targets. MYCIN was designed to carry out medical diagnosis within a very limited sphere.
Performance targets that could be employed would include

- time taken to produce diagnosis
- percentage of results agreeing with a group of human experts
- number of sales to doctors.

Expert systems have been validated in this way for a number of years, e.g. an evaluation of MYCIN has been published by Duda and Shortliffe (1983).

These targets relate to 'match-to-needs' quality or 'fitness for purpose'. We must also set performance targets for the technical aspects of quality, which thus far have been regarded as 'match-to-spec'. It has already been pointed out that one

A ╲ B	R	E	S	I	U	M	A	P	T	C B	E T	U F
Reliability	✕	–	+	**+**	◎	◎	◎	◎	**−**	◎	◎	**+**
Efficiency	–	✕	–	◎	**−**	–	**−**	**−**	**−**	◎	**−**	–
Security	◎	◎	✕	+	**−**	◎	◎	◎	**−**	◎	◎	**−**
Integrity	**+**	◎	+	✕	◎	◎	–	◎	**−**	◎	+	◎
Usability	**+**	◎	**−**	◎	✕	◎	◎	–	**−**	◎	**+**	◎
Maintainability	◎	**−**	–	◎	–	✕	**+**	◎	**−**	◎	◎	◎
Adaptability	◎	**−**	–	◎	–	**+**	✕	◎	**−**	◎	◎	◎
Portability	◎	**−**	**−**	◎	**−**	+	**+**	✕	**−**	◎	**+**	**−**
Timeliness	**−**	**−**	**−**	**−**	**−**	+	◎	**−**	✕	◎	+	**−**
Cost/Benefit	**+**	**+**	◎	◎	**+**	**+**	**+**	**+**	**+**	✕	**+**	**+**
Ease of Transition	◎	◎	**−**	+	◎	**+**	**+**	**+**	**−**	◎	✕	◎
User Friendliness	**+**	**+**	**−**	**+**	**+**	◎	◎	◎	**+**	◎	**+**	✕

Tab. 6.5 Quality interrelationships.

of the problems with expert systems is the evolving nature of the specification. However, it is possible to set targets for basic technical parameters at the start of the project. These performance targets should be built into the specification at the start and compromises may then only be made by negotiation between the designers and the clients, resulting in a revised specification.

Performance targets for the quality criteria of the new framework are suggested below:

(a) Reliability. The reliability of systems from the users point of view is concerned with three things:
- How often does it go wrong?
- How long is it unavailable?
- Is any information lost at recovery?

These may be measured respectively as

$$\text{Mean Time To Failure} = \text{Total Time Period/Number of failures}$$

$$\text{Time Unavailable (\%)} = (\text{Time Unavailable/Total Time}) \times 100$$

$$\text{Information Loss(\%)} = \text{Information before (bytes)/Information after (bytes)}$$

(b) Efficiency. The key here is to define the critical tasks and the critical resources. The critical resources by the operator to carry out the critical tasks can be monitored, e.g. if staff time is the critical resource, the elapsed time taken is the best measure of efficiency. On the other hand, if the computer disk storage is critical, then the percentage of disk space required to carry out the task is the best measure available.

(c) Security. This may be measured as the resource cost expended to solve problems caused by unauthorized activity. This resource cost may be appear in a number of ways, e.g. staff time to recover system (time), loss of information (bytes).

(d) Integrity. Integrity may be measured as the resource cost expended to solve problems caused by inconsistencies within the system. This may be measured in terms of staff time employed to fix problems and user time wasted.

(e) Usability. Usability may be measured in terms of user surveys as apparently IBM do. However, it may also be assessed in terms of calls upon support staff, e.g., number of requests for help, support staff time expended.

(f) Maintainability. Maintainability may most simply be measured by the resources expended in terms of time and cost in keeping a system up and running over a period of time.

(g) Adaptability. Adaptability may be measured in the same way as maintainability, the resources expended in adapting the system to meet new requirements over a period of time.

(h) Portability. This may be measured according to Gilb's measure (see above).

(i) Timeliness. Timeliness may be assessed in terms of the costs of non-delivery. These will include indicators such as staff time and lost sales. It may also be assessed in terms of days departure from the date agreed with client.

(j) Cost-Benefit Efficiency. This may be measured in simple financial terms. The costs of installing and maintaining the system are weighed against the assessment of business benefits

(k) Ease of Transition. The ease of transition may be assessed in terms of staff time expended. The effectiveness of transition may be assessed in terms of the quality of the resulting system particularly the area of integrity.

(l) Userfriendliness. This property may be measured in terms of the effect upon the effectiveness of the user. The measure of userfriendliness in business terms is the productivity of the user.

It is important to consider these criteria as a whole. The measures are designed to work in this way. For example, the way that maintainability is measured means that a low cost ('high quality') figure could be obtained by inaction on the part of staff. However, this would be reflected in the reliability and integrity measures.

The performance targets may then be represented graphically using a profiling technique. This approach has been adopted for use in personnel profiling by PA in their PAPI (Proficiency and Preference Inventory) scheme. This scheme uses twenty measurements characterized under seven headings. The scores are plotted on a linear scale from the centre outwards. A schematic profile of this type is shown in Fig. 6.8. Personnel schemes such as PAPI do not make an intuitive leap between the area enclosed by the profile and an overall measure. The use of a PAPI-style profile where such an intuitive link is made, e.g. to display an overall measure of quality, is subject to the following limitations:

- The area is proportional to the square of the overall quantity.
- The area is affected by the order of components plotted.

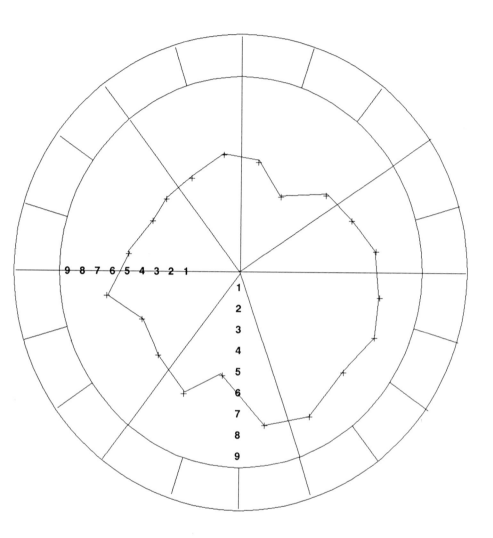

Fig. 6.8 A schematic PAPI profile.

- The area is affected by the number of measures available for each characteristic.

Care is needed if the area of the profile is to reflect the overall quality of the system.

The following alternative scheme, shown in Fig. 6.9, is suggested by the author to maximise the comparability of the profiles. The profile is plotted within a circle. Each criteria is allocated equal area within the circle. Within each principal sector, each measure is then allocated an equal share of that sector. Thus if we represent software quality in terms of the twelve criteria of the model and there are three measures associated with reliability, the area allocated to each measure will be a sector defining an angle of 10° at the centre of the circle. The scale runs from the outside into the centre. The profile is plotted from the circumference to the profile points and back between each point, within a polygon.

In this fashion, the area depends principally upon the value plotted. However, a small correction is required due to edge effects arising when the number of measures associated with each criteria is different. The underlying mathematical theory has been presented elsewhere (Gillies and Hart, 1991). In practice, the profiles are drawn by a computer tool, which provides the user with an accurate representation of the data provided in a convenient and accessible way.

Plotted in this manner, the profile has the following properties:

- The area of the profile depends linearly upon the values of the performance parameters.
- The area of the profile is independent of the order of measures.
- The area of the profile is independent of the number of measures associated with each characteristic, i.e. the area arising from a criteria with one associated measure is the same as the area arising from one with n associated measures providing the mean value of the measures is equivalent to that of the single measure.

6.4.2 Future work

The practical assessment of the quality of expert systems is still in its infancy, as systems move into commercial and manufacturing environments. Many of the developments in information systems targeted at improving information systems quality have implications for expert systems. Quality control procedures in the past have often been based around a sequential waterfall lifecycle model of development ill-suited to expert systems. With the growth in popularity of evolutionary development procedures, research into new methods of quality management and assessment is ongoing by the author and other researchers in the field.

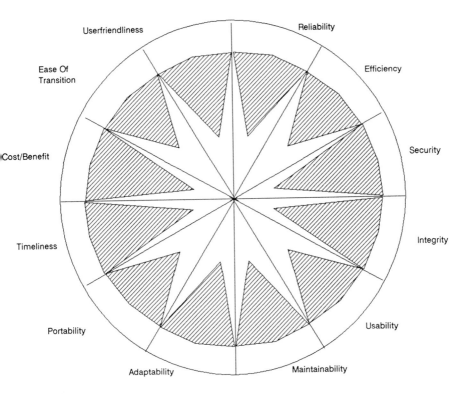

Fig. 6.9 Quality Profile.

6.5 Further reading

This short book provides a good survey of the literature up to 1987. It also reports the results of an NCC Anglo-German research project, including the MQ model: Watts, R.(1987) *Measuring Software Quality*, NCC Publications.

Sections of this great tome contain useful reading about evaluating software quality, and more recent references than Watts' book. Chapters 1,10,14,15,17,20–23,27,29 and 30 (in fact, most of the book) are particularly useful: Sommerville, I.(1989) *Software Engineering* (3rd edn.) Addison–Wesley.

This book although a few years old now, remains one of the best practical guides to the practice of Quality Assurance:
Perry,W. E. (1983) *Effective Methods of EDP Quality Assurance*, Prentice–Hall.

CHAPTER SEVEN

Case Study I: The JKBS methodology

Software engineers may consider expert systems, however reluctantly, when conventional systems run out of steam. This methodology was born out of just such a scenario. The methodology seeks to combine human, algorithmic and knowledge-based contributions in situations where algorithms prove inadequate. The methodology is used to construct a system used for fringe analysis in an image processing system limited by hardware.

This chapter describes the methodology developed and some of the resulting systems.

7.1 The problem

The aim of the project was to automate the technique of photoelastic stress analysis, which remains one of the most useful and accurate stress analysis techniques available. One of the principal drawbacks of the technique is the time and expertise required to analyze the fringe patterns produced. This project investigated the application of image processing techniques to the analysis of photoelastic fringe patterns.

Photoelastic fringe patterns may be viewed under polarized light when an object is stressed. The interested reader is recommended to read Hendry (1966) to discover more about photoelasticity. For our purposes, it is sufficient to note that the resulting pattern is an interference pattern similar to that observed when oil lies on water giving rise to a coloured pattern. Photoelastic patterns may be observed in colour, or monochrome. Generally, monochromatic light is used for quantitative work. The pattern may be captured using a video camera, digitized and fed into a computer for processing (Fig. 7.1).

The analysis of photoelastic fringe patterns may be considered in two phases. Phase one consists of resolving the optical fringe pattern whilst Phase two is the analysis of the resolved pattern. Phase one is amenable in theory to an algorithmic solution . However, the project was constrained by budget considerations, and with the existing hardware only about 80% of the information was available from an algorithmic solution. Improving the hardware was an option subject to the law of diminishing returns and unlikely to provide sufficient improvement to justify the expense. The alternative approach was to use knowledge about the fringe pattern to reconstruct the image. Phase two is generally done by the operator using relatively scarce expertise in a time-consuming process. This scenario suggests that a KBS solution may be appropriate. The integrated approach is suggested by the combination of image processing and knowledge about the pattern. A further possibility for integration is the inclusion of the user for visual tasks not requiring

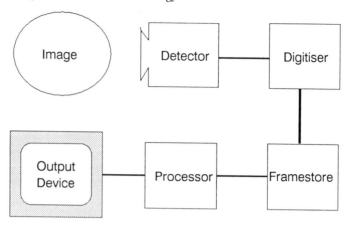

Fig. 7.1 An image processing system (schematic).

specific expertise. In spite of much research in the computer vision area, the human eye remains a very cost-effective, efficient and reliable solution in many cases.

An integrated solution offers a number of advantages:
- It provides a solution for the whole problem.
- It allows maximum exploitation of each technique and resource available.
- It is likely to be more cost-effective than enhancing hardware.
- It allows analysis to be carried out without specific expertise.

A methodology was developed to tackle problems requiring the integration of algorithmic image processing, knowledge and human vision, known as the Joint Knowledge-Based System (JKBS) approach.

7.2 The JKBS methodology

The JKBS methodology seeks to combine human and machine expertise with low level image processing methods. It seeks to formalise the interrelationship of the agencies, and to integrate all three in a system where the whole is greater than the sum of the parts. The role of the methodology is to provide a strategy for determining the best method for the specific problem under investigation: by taking the approach a step back from the method to the methodology, a number of advantages ensue. An opportunity is provided for the design of genuinely flexible problem-centred methods. This means methods from conventional software can be integrated with the KBS approach. The role of the user may be reassessed: even a novice user has much to offer in terms of perceptual knowledge.

Developers of KBS would traditionally assume that knowledge should be explicit and rule-based. For problems in graphics and image processing, this may not be possible and even where it is possible, it may not provide the optimum solution. In determining a new integrated methodology for problem-solving in the graphical and image processing domain, a return to basics was envisaged: how could the knowledge available be best employed in a solution to the problem?

The JKBS methodology is summarized in Fig. 7.2. The adopted approach has been to start with the problem. The key to providing the desired features of robustness, clarity and ease of modification is perceived to lie in structuring the task to be modelled as a series of sub-tasks. Given a thorough analysis and

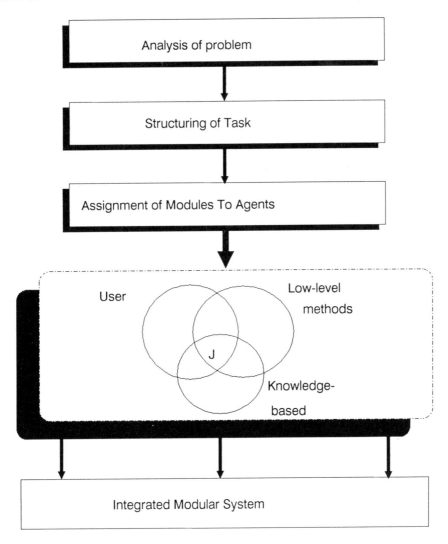

Fig. 7.2 Summary of the JKBS methodology.

understanding of the problem and the intended users, the aim has been to design a system which carries out each sub-task by means of whichever single technique or combination of techniques is most effective. This allows the implementation of each sub-task to be optimised. Each sub-task is represented by a module of the program. Each module must be independent and this favours the use of structured languages such as C or Pascal, which also allow rapid numerical computation.

The key stage in a successful implementation based upon the methodology is the structuring of the task and the subsequent division into subtasks. The approach for this stage of the development is based upon a 'traditional' knowledge elicitation exercise. The results of low-level processing are given to a stress analyst with a knowledge of photoelasticity and he is asked to carry out the task of completing the pattern. The effectiveness of this type of exercise has been questioned in the past, since the view has been expressed (Dreyfus, 1985) that expertise cannot be modelled adequately in terms of rules, so that the attempt is at best futile and, at worst, misleading. The experience from such work in the past has often been that the expertise is expressed in terms of examples and anecdotes rather than rules. In this work the anticipated result, therefore, is not a set of rules, but rather a set of sub-tasks, which may each be considered separately by the system designer.

The methodology may be distinguished by several features:

(a) The method is determined by the problem or class of problems to be investigated.

(b) The division of labour and choice of method is critical and is viewed as an early and essential part of the knowledge elicitation process.

(c) The aim of the knowledge elicitation is not to wholly encompass human expertise within a set of rules, but to structure the task and thereby provide a structure for the solution.

(d) Knowledge representation is considered to be broader than a rule-base. Since the primary application area of the methodology has been in graphical problems, the specific needs of graphical knowledge representation are accommodated.

(e) The user is regarded as a useful resource, especially as a visual detector. Where a human user with little expertise can make an effective contribution to a task rapidly and efficiently, such a contribution is incorporated into the system.

(f) Use of heuristic rule-based models is made only when it is most efficient so to do. Traditional methods such as numerical analysis are introduced to solve problems best suited to such an approach.

g) The software is constructed in modular form.

h) In order to maximise the effectiveness of the user, emphasis is placed upon providing a helpful interface. The role of explanation is considered to be determined best by the problem domain. A graphical domain suggests a graphical explanation facility.

Particular attention was paid to two areas, explanation and structuredness of code. In order to build confidence in the conclusions, and allow for quality control, most expert systems have an explanation facility: it is generally assumed that the user will require explanation of the programme's line of reasoning in response to a query 'Why?'. This tends to be achieved by outputting the rules which the system has recently used in an accessible and adaptable form. However, such rules can be difficult to understand from the user's point of view and may not constitute an explanation. Current research suggests user dissatisfaction with current computer explanation (Berry and Broadbent, 1987)).

In the image processing domain considered here, a simple text message cannot be construed as an explanation. The alternative, implemented here is to report all operations to the screen as they happen in a graphical manner. It is felt that text, beyond a simple prompt message, would merely serve to confuse. The Joint KBS approach is characterized by an attempt to be driven by user's needs and not current computer thinking. Good graphics should be self-explanatory as the designers of man-machine interfaces based around graphical icons have shown.

Transparency and ease of modification are generally considered to be highly desirable. However, in practice, an expert system of considerable depth and complexity can rarely be made up of wholly independent rules, so that altering one rule may have unforeseen consequences elsewhere in the inference network. The need to structure expert systems like XCON (McDermott, 1985) bears this out.

The JKBS approach leads to a modular approach, separating tasks and modelling them in different ways. This, together with judicious use of a language such as PASCAL leads to a system with good transparency.

7.3 Two resulting systems

The JKBS approach has been used to develop two systems to analyze photoelastic fringe patterns.

7.3.1 System to analyze a disc under diametral compression

The first investigation concerns the image of a fringe pattern taken from a disc under diametral compression. This is of interest because this geometry is used to calibrate sheets of photoelastic material for quantitative work. The starting point for the knowledge-based image restoration process is the results from low-level processing (Fig. 7.3).

The results from the knowledge elicitation suggest the following stages are required in the process of image restoration:

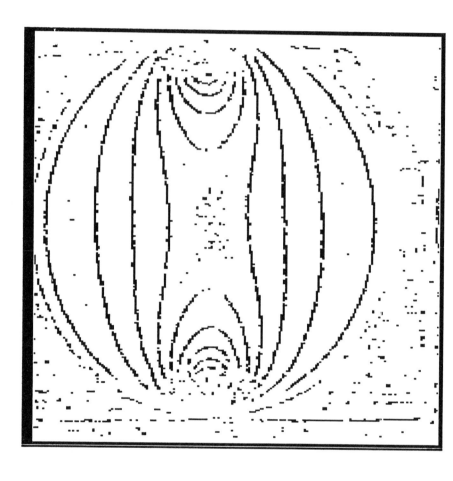

Fig. 7.3 Results from low-level processing.

(a) identification of the disc geometry,
(b) identification of the area of good resolution,
(c) identification of fringes within this area,
(d) identification of possible fringes outside this area,
(e) extrapolation of fringes into the area of unreliable data,
(f) comparison of extrapolated data with digitized image.

The next stage of the analysis is the allocation of the tasks to the following agencies: human, computer heuristics, low-level computer methods. The allocation used in the implementation is summarized in Tab. 7.1.

The implemented system proceeds in the following manner. The system first requires two pieces of information from the user; the disc boundary and the area where visually good fringe discrimination may be seen. The user enters the disc boundary as four data points using the mouse; top of the disc, bottom of the disc, left edge of the disc, right edge of the disc (Fig. 7.4).

The system takes the mean of the four points entered and calculates the centre of the disc. From this, a mean radius is calculated and the result shown on the screen. The user is then given the choice of accepting the result or re-entering the data. The area where good fringe discrimination is entered as a rectangle superimposed upon the disc (Fig. 7.5).

This is only an approximate measure, and the results are not particularly sensitive to this data. The system then considers the data within the region assigned as showing good fringe discrimination. The information from this region is combined with knowledge of the fringe pattern to produce a model of the fringe pattern. The points detected by the image processing may be regarded as an information base. These points are grouped into collections of points corresponding to fringes. The fringe centres are allocated using splines fitted to the midpoint of the regression line found for each group of points. The splines are fitted subject to the following constraints:

(a) each fringe shows four-fold symmetry about the centre of the disc,
(b) each fringe passes through the points of loading,
(c) the gradient at the points of loading is zero,
(d) the gradient at the horizontal diameter is infinite.

The spline marking the fringe centre is swept through the full circle using polar co-ordinates. These fringes are used to construct further fringes according to a model pattern. The fitted results are, therefore, approximate. However, they do not contain spurious features. The next stage is to compare the fitted results with the results from the area where the data is unreliable. These results are characterized by accuracy of position, but with spurious features present. The aim is to combine accuracy with freedom from spuriae.

Before comparison can be made, the fringes must be allocated a fringe order. Fringe ordering is required to turn a series of lines into a representation of an

Task	Sub Task	Agency		
		U	K	B
Define Symmetry	Select Shape	X		
	Enter boundary	X		
	Find radius,centre		X	
Grade Information	Low fringes		X	
	High fringes		X	
	Useful area.	X		
Fringe Discrimation	Lowlevel IP			X
	Fringe tracing		X	
	Smoothing			X
Geometrical Knowledge	Construct Model		X	
Results Comparison	Analysis res.			X
	Model res.			X
	Comparison	X		
	Remove spuriae	X		
	Insert missing fringes	X		
	Extrapolate			X

Tab. 7.1 Task allocation for disc analysis.

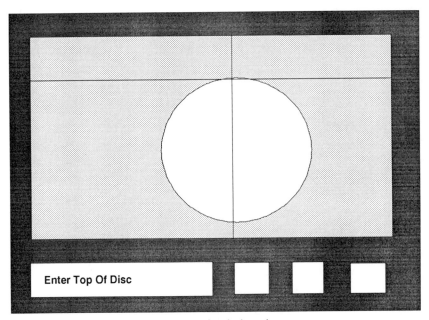

Fig. 7.4 Entering the boundary.

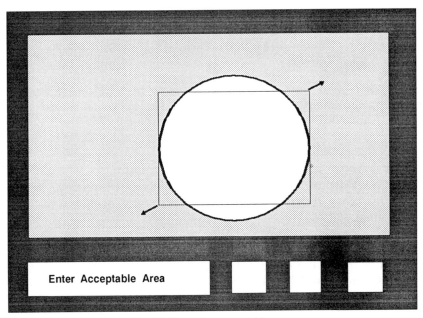

Fig. 7.5 Entry of an acceptable area.

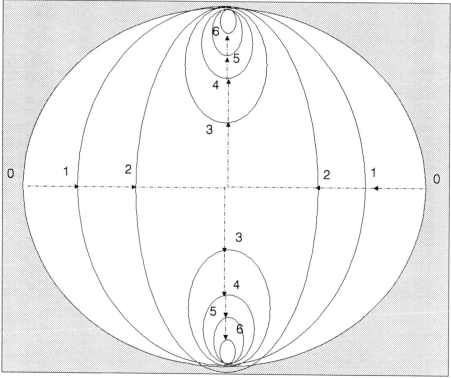

Fig 7.6 Fringe ordering.

optical fringe pattern, from which the stresses may be calculated. This may be achieved by the computer, using represented knowledge about the pattern geometry. The process, illustrated in Fig. 7.6., is based upon three pieces of knowledge:

(a) The zeroth order fringe is found at the edge of the disc.
(b) The fringe order increases incrementally until the centre is reached.
(c) From the centre the fringe order is increased incrementally towards the top and bottom.

The comparison of the two sets of results is carried out by the user with the help of a graphical interface. The process consists of two stages, elimination of spurious fringes illustrated in Fig. 7.7, and insertion of missing fringes illustrated in Fig. 7.8.

7.3.2 A system to analyze beams under bending

The second case-study is based upon a family of case-studies using images from patterns in beams, notched and straight, loaded in pure bending. The models were

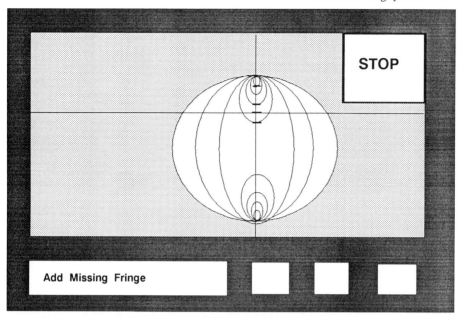

Fig. 7.7 Entering missing fringes.

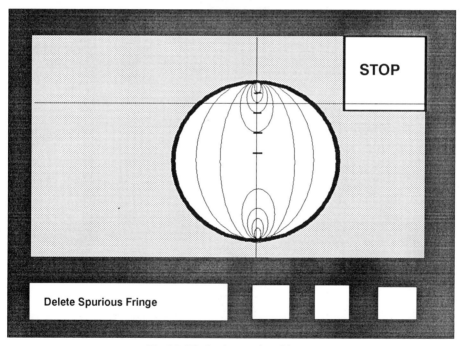

Fig. 7.8 Eliminating spurious fringes.

examined using essentially the same apparatus as used in the disc study. The starting-point for image restoration is the results from low-level image processing. A typical input image is illustrated in Fig. 7.9.

The knowledge elicitation exercise suggests that the image restoration process may be divided into the following stages:

(a) identification of the beam boundary,
(b) identification of the zeroth order fringe,
(c) labelling of pixels exterior to the boundary,
(d) thinning to completion,
(e) removal of artefacts from thinning process,
(f) assignment of fringe orders,
(g) completion of incomplete fringes,
(h) completion of pattern.

The next stage of the analysis is the allocation of the tasks to the previously described agencies: human, computer heuristics, low-level computer methods. The allocation used in the implementation is summarized in Tab. 7.2.

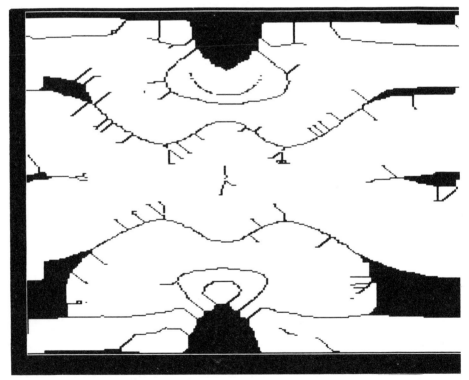

Fig. 7.9 Results from low-level processing.

Task	Sub Task	Agency		
		U	K	B
Define Geometry	Enter Corners	X		
	Enter Notch	X		
	Enter Zero	X		
Identify Exterior Pixels	Pixel Identification		X	
Intelligent Thinning	Thinning Procedure		X	X
	Removal of artefacts	X	X	
Fringe Ordering	Pixel Ordering		X	
	Fringe Check		X	
Pattern Completion	Completion of partial fringes	X	X	
	Extrapolation to limit		X	

Tab. 7.2 Task allocation for beam problems.

The implemented procedure consists of four broad stages: geometrical data input, modified thinning, fringe order assignment, pattern completion. The system requires three pieces of information from the user: the position of the zeroth order fringe, the corners of the beam and the edges of the notch, if present. The data is entered by use of the mouse, whose position is shown on the screen by means of a crosshair (Fig. 7.10).

The position of the zeroth order fringe is readily determined by the non-expert user by examining the pattern under coloured light where it will show up as black in a coloured fringe pattern. It should also be noted that in this implementation all the positions indicated by the user are taken as approximate by the computer. The computer uses the entered position as a guide, the final position being determined by rule-based procedures. This exemplifies the principle of optimising the use of each agency. The user can quickly identify the approximate position and the computer can quickly identify the precise location within a small region.

Once the geometry is established, an pseudo 'intelligent' thinning procedure is employed. Thinning algorithms are designed to reduce areas to a single centre line and are applied to binary images. The basic algorithm used within the procedure described by Zhang and Suen (1984), modified by Lu and Wang (1986), is summarized in Fig. 7.11.

Enter Left Hand Corner...

Fig. 7.10 Entering beam boundary data.

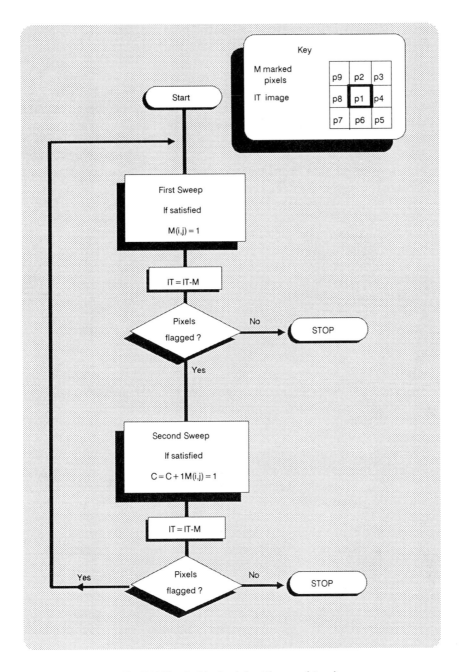

Fig. 7.11 Simple thinning (after Zhang and Suen).

The algorithm is applied to every contour point, that is every dark pixel having at least one light neighbour. The pixel is flagged for deletion if the following conditions are satisfied:

(1) the number of non-zero neighbours is between 2 and 6,
(2) the number of ordered light-dark transitions around the pixel is 1,
(3a) $p2.p4.p6 = 0$ and $p4.p6.p8 = 0$ where pn is defined as in Fig. 7.11 overleaf, and a dark pixel is assigned a value 1, and a light pixel value 0.

If (1),(2) and (3a) are satisfied, the pixel is flagged for deletion. When all pixels have been considered, the flagged pixels are deleted. The procedure is repeated, but condition (3a) now becomes:
(3b) $p2.p4.p8 = 0$ and $p2.p6.p8 = 0$

Once all the relevant pixels are flagged, they are deleted. The algorithm thus consists of four stages:
(i)   flag all pixels satisfying (1),(2),(3a),
(ii) delete all flagged pixels,
(iii) flag all pixels satisfying (1),(2),(3b),
(iv) delete all flagged pixels.

The process is iterative, and proceeds to completion when no further pixels are flagged. The problem for use in our system is that because the algorithm is not 'intelligent' it cannot distinguish fringe lines from other features, notably the boundary. It is also prone to introducing 'tails'. If we are to protect boundaries in our image and keep our fringe lines free from tails, we must introduce intelligence, either represented on the machine or call on the user for assistance.

The solution adopted is to utilise thinning within an overall system context which includes preprocessing, human perception and the use of rules. The modifications to the thinning process are concerned with tackling the two types of defects. Since they are essentially artefacts of the thinning process, specific knowledge is available about their cause and effect. They are, therefore, easier to deal with than defects arising from limitations in pixel or spatial resolution, or defects inherent in the image which will be case-dependent.

It   consists of several distinct stages: pre-processing, thresholding, initial thinning, identification of the boundary, ternary labelling, thinning to completion, removal of common defects. Pre-processing consists of median filtering over a 9-pixel neighbourhood. This is intended to minimise irregularities at the thresholding stage which results in 'tails' in the processed image. After thresholding, the image is partially thinned. This aids the user in the next stage of boundary identification. The user is required to enter sufficient data to uniquely define the boundary. In the case of the notched beam, this is four corners and the edges of the notches. The user is only required to approximately identify the locations, the computer using rule-based procedures to accurately determine the positions of the features.

After the boundary is identified, the computer labels the points exterior to the boundary as value 2. Since the thinning algorithm only effects 'dark' pixels, i.e. those recorded as value 1, the exterior points are left intact, preventing boundary erosion. The thinning is now allowed to proceed to completion as in the original algorithm.

After thinning, the result is characterized by a small number of defects, arising from the thinning process. Because these defects arise from the thinning process, they are identifiable, and may be corrected. The common defects are gaps in the fringe centre lines, centre lines disconnected from the boundary and 'tails'. The approach adopted in cleaning up the image is the same for each defect. A joint procedure is adopted, in which the user locates the approximate position of the defect. The computer identifies the exact position of the defect, and corrects for it using rule-based procedures.

Novel use is made of the thinning algorithm in the plugging of gaps in the fringe centre lines. The user identifies the approximate position of the gap on the screen using the mouse. The computer checks the selected pixel does not lie on a fringe centre line, then looks for the nearest ends of fringe centre lines. A square is shaded with maximum dimensions equal to the gap between the centre line fragments.

The shaded region is then thinned down using the thinning algorithm to produce a complete fringe. The use of thinning in this way provides a rapid method of gap filling which takes account of the directional information present in the centre line fragments adjacent to the gap. It also produces compact and consistent code since the thinning algorithm may be called in from elsewhere.

The other defects are dealt with similarly, the user providing approximate location of the defect, and the computer finding the exact location and correcting appropriately. After correction, the thinning part of the procedure is complete. The results are then analysed by a rule-based procedure which embodies knowledge of fringe ordering within a pattern. The fringe centre lines are first assigned fringe orders and then the pattern is completed by analysis for missing and incomplete fringes.

The modified thinning procedure builds upon the features of the original algorithm. The results from the new procedure have been most encouraging within the specific problem domain addressed. The procedure shows good speed performance and robustness to noise.

By modelling knowledge about the defects of the algorithm rather than the pattern, the use of knowledge is simplified. Similarly, by making use of human visual perception to approximately locate features, the use of computer knowledge for defect correction is simplified and accelerated.

The modified thinning procedure summarized in Fig. 7.12, represents the synthesis of the original algorithm, human perception and rule-based computer models of human knowledge. The end-result represents a result unattainable by low-level techniques alone, without resort to greater pixel and spatial resolutions with a consequent penalty in terms of computation and expense.

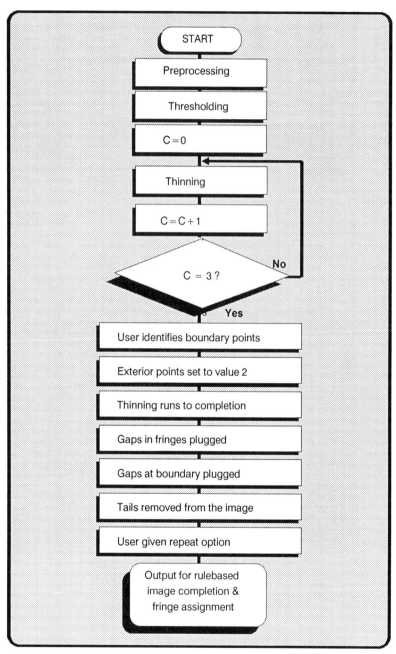

Fig. 7.12 Intelligent thinning.

The thinning procedure produces a ternary image which is labelled according to the following system: fringe centres (0), background within model (1), exterior pixels (2). The pattern is incomplete and contains both incomplete and missing fringe centre lines.

The image array is now multiplied by negative 1, to facilitate the labelling of the fringe centre lines. Thus exterior pixels are labelled as -2, interior background pixels as -1, and the fringe centre pixels as 0. Each pixel labelled zero is now assigned an integer fringe order by a rule-based procedure.

The path between each zero-labelled pixel and the zeroth order fringe is considered. Each time a fringe is crossed, the notional fringe order is altered. If the fringe encountered is part of a fringe already encountered, the fringe order is decremented, otherwise the fringe order is incremented as in Fig. 7.13.

Once all the zero-labelled pixels have been assigned, all the pixels with a positive integer assigned to them i.e. the pixels on fringe centre lines are checked to ensure that all such adjacent pixels share the same value. This ensures that the fringes are consistently labelled.

The results at this stage are still incomplete. The region where incomplete resolution is most probable are those regions where the fringe orders are highest. The fringe pattern is completed in two stages. First the completion of incomplete fringes. The user identifies the position of incomplete fringes (Fig. 7.14) and the computer combines this data with the shape from the highest complete fringe to produce a new complete fringe.

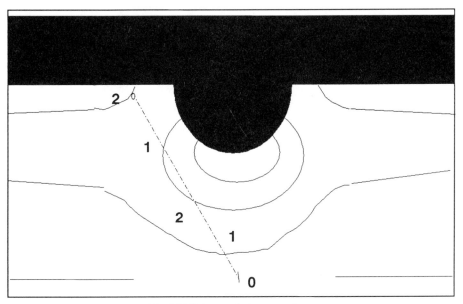

Fig. 7.13 Fringe ordering procedure.

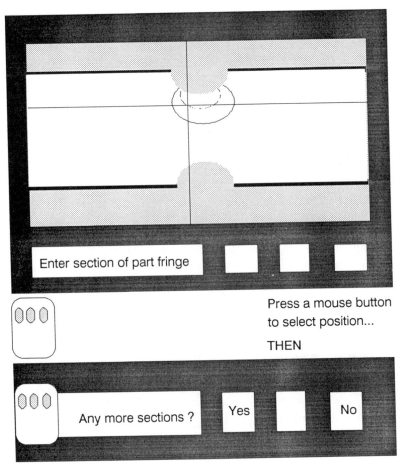

Fig. 7.14 Fringe completion procedure.

After this stage is complete, the computer calculates the fringe order distribution in the area of highest fringe order. The computer then predicts where the next highest fringe should lie. The system incorporates rules to tell the computer if this acceptable and if so, it is added to the pattern.

7.4   Some results from the systems

The completed disc pattern is illustrated in Fig. 7.15. The use of rules allows the scope of the technique to be extended from simple image restoration to include fringe order assignment.

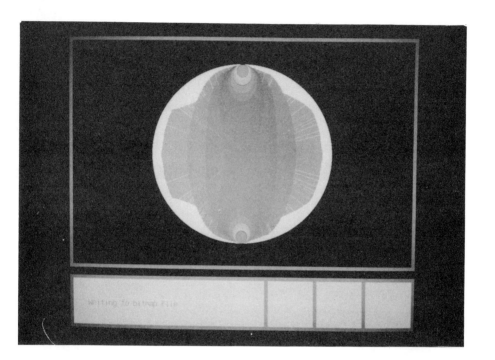

Fig. 7.15 Results from disc.

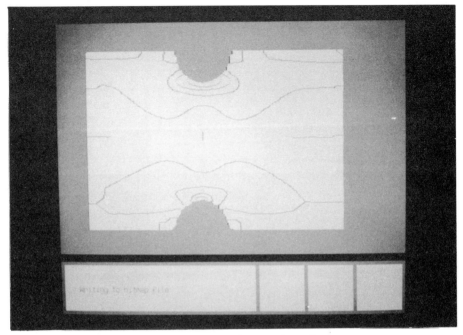

Fig. 7.16 Beam results : experimental.

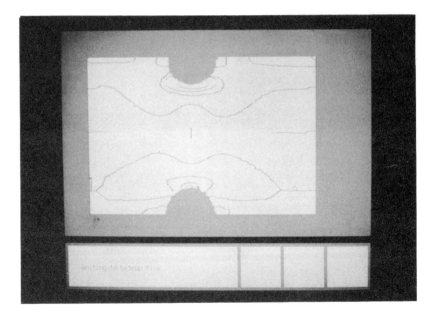

Fig. 7.17 Beam results with added noise.

Several beam problems have been analysed. The technique has proved relatively robust with respect to random additive noise. This is shown in Figs. 7.16 and 7.17 where the results from an experimental image, and one with artificially added Gaussian noise are compared.

7.5 Further reading

For further information about this work, the reader is pointed towards the following research papers.

These two papers describe the JKBS methodology in greater detail.

Gillies, A. C. and Hart. A. E (1989a) Using knowledge-based ideas in image processing: A Case Study in Human Computer Interaction, *Research and Development in Expert Systems V, Proc. ES'88, Brighton, UK*, CUP.

Gillies, A. C and Hart, A. E (1989b) Using Knowledge to enhance the scope and efficiency of image processing in fringe analysis, *Proc IEEE/SPIE Applications of artificial intelligence* **VII**, *Florida, USA*, SPIE vol no 1095.

The full results from the beam and disc case-studies are presented here.

Gillies,A .C. , Keskin, O. Telfer, D. J. and Whiteley, K. (1988) The use of a priori knowledge in the analysis of fringe patterns, *Proc. Int. Conf. Opt. Eng, (EPS/SPIE), Hamburg*, SPIE vol 1010.

Case Study II: 'Organization for combat'

Whether we like it or not, much impetus for research comes from the military. The system described here was required to be an expert system capable of conforming to American military specifications, running in Ada on a battlefield 8086 PC, noted more for its ability to fall out of a plane than for its processing power. It is notable for its creative use of an AI tool in the construction of a system conforming to classic software engineering rules.

This chapter describes the work undertaken, the underlying philosophy and some of the consequent lessons.

8.1 Introduction

Concern about software quality has led to the introduction of strict standards for both Total Quality Management (TQM) of software development and for the software and hardware systems themselves. The American DoD lays down standards relating to most aspects of software design. Current requirements for decision support systems targeted at military use, are software written in Ada, running on hardware designed first to be dropped out of planes and run computer programs a poor second. This presents a number of challenges to the expert system designer.

(a) The specified software environment. The specified software environment is Ada. It is not an easy language in which to implement an expert system. It lacks the data structures and knowledge representation schemes which form the basis of most AI development environments.

(b) The specified hardware. Expert systems are traditionally inefficient, and run on powerful workstations where their inefficiency can be overlooked. The required target hardware is positively inefficient. The combination of inefficient software with inefficient hardware is potentially crippling.

The example described here shows how one company set about designing and implementing a decision support system for organization for combat (OFC) within the constraints laid down by the requirements of the military application. It describes how they used both AI and conventional technology to overcome the constraints listed above. Neither technology could provide a solution by itself.

The approach adopted has implications for other applications where expert systems are required in situations where external requirements render a conventional expert system unsuitable.

8.2 The problem

The problem to be tackled by the company was the provision of decision support for organization for combat. The need arises from the DoD's requirement to defeat a numerically superior attack force by use of force multiplication through a complex system of sensors, weapons and control and command systems. The result of all these systems being available to a soldier is a severe case of information overload. This project was intended to provide machine support for the decision making process, in order to prevent the response time from the human decision maker becoming too long.

The project was undertaken by the Magnavox Electronic Systems Co. and the work has been published by Dunkelberger (1989). The problem was considered to be suitable for decision support for five reasons, detailed below:

- The manual process was tedious and long-winded.
- The knowledge was readily available.
- The problem had well-defined boundaries and appeared tractable.
- Validation was possible.
- Delivery and distribution hardware was available.

The system was designed in such a way as to become a module in a larger system.

8.2.1. The computer problem

The computing problem faced by the designer represents the classic mismatch between software engineering and AI. The designer wishes to use the range of AI tools and data structures available to him in order to maximise the effectiveness of the solution. The product, however, was required to be delivered in tightly specified Ada, which conforms to US DoD standards.

The in-house development environment is the ART tool (Artificial Reasoning Tool, supplied by the Inference Corporation), running on Sun workstations and Gigamos LISP machines. It delivers a highly interactive development environment dedicated to an incremental design process, similar to those based upon the RUDE cycle, discussed in Chapter 4, generally considered to be most appropriate for expert system development.

The customer specified delivery environment consists of inefficient ruggedized hardware supporting the required Ada environment consisting of separate editors, compilers and debuggers constrained by a sequential specification and design strategy, derived from a very traditional waterfall lifecycle model. Some workers have gone so far as to state that it is not possible to implement an AI system in a such a rigid environment.

DEVELOPMENT   **DELIVERY**

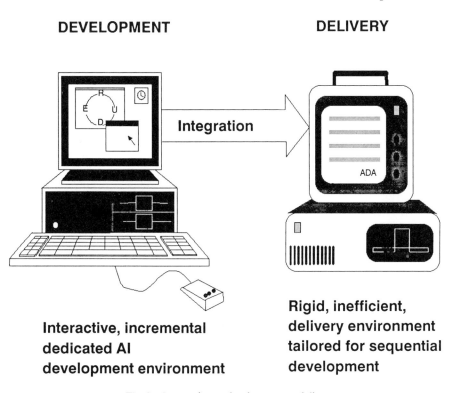

Integration

Interactive, incremental
dedicated AI
development environment

Rigid, inefficient,
delivery environment
tailored for sequential
development

Fig. 8.1 Integration as development to delivery.

Integration in this case is concerned with bridging the gap between the AI development environment and the Ada delivery environment (Fig. 8.1).

Dunkelberger suggests there are three possible approaches, which may be seen to differ slightly from the three levels of integration suggested in Chapter 1, since the aim of integration is not to extend the scope of the system but rather to deliver the system in a more acceptable form.

(a) *Port concept alone.* A prototype system is developed within the AI environment. From this, only the structure and the knowledge representation is taken, and implementation starts again from scratch.

(b) *Port concept and software.* If a common language were available in both environments then the system could be ported complete from development to implementation. Unfortunately, this is not the case.

(c) *Deliver militarized version of the development prototype.* This path assumes only the form of the prototype will be changed to meet the customer requirements.

The options (a) to (c) show a decreasing risk from a development view. However, given current technology, the feasibility of a successful implementation also decreases.

The alternative is developing within the rigid Ada delivery environment. The problems associated with trying to develop an AI system directly in accordance with the military requirements are, in practical terms, prohibitive. The rigid development cycle is likely to lead to a product which is 'flawless, it just happens to be the wrong product' (Dunkelberger, *ibid*).

The approach adopted, therefore, by the designer was to design a prototype within the AI environment and then re-code the system from scratch.

8.2.2. The military problem

Military operations may generally be considered as a number of phases (Fig. 8.2). OFC may be regarded as a phased matching problem. Each phase is analyzed separately, but there are constraints acting upon each phase from the preceding and subsequent phases. Each phase may be regarded as a discrete unit of time (Fig. 8.3).

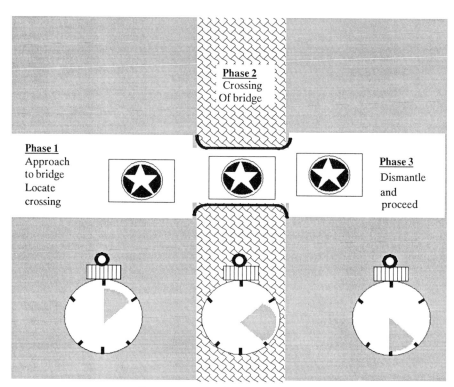

Fig. 8.2 Example of a phased operation.

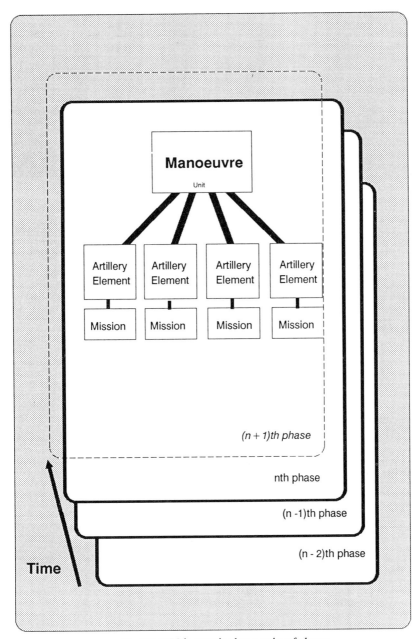

Fig. 8.3 OFC is organized as a series of phases.

The elements to be matched are manoeuvre units and field artillery units. Manoeuvre elements are dealt with at the brigade level. During an operation, they are located in sectors, and one of these sectors is associated with the main effort. They may take up an offensive or defensive posture. This posture may change from phase to phase or from sector to sector within a phase. They may take one of three roles: committed, supporting or reserve.

Within each phase, manoeuvre elements must be matched to field artillery units. Each manoeuvre element may have more than one artillery element associated with it, i.e. there is a one-to-many relationship between manoeuvre elements and artillery elements. Field artillery elements may have one of four missions at any one time: direct support, reinforcing, general support reinforcing, and general support. The artillery units have different sorts of weapons, which make them suitable for different missions. The elements employed in the OFC aid and their possible roles and values are illustrated in Fig. 8.4.

Further constraints arise in practice because habitual associations arising from artillery units training together. These associations become de facto assignments in the OFC process.

The basic doctrine laid down for organization for combat is found in the US Army military field manuals. The section relating to OFC is only six pages long. However, the generality of the guidelines reinforces the need for effective decision support. Five basic tenets are provided, listed in Tab. 8.1.

These tenets provide some immediate considerations for decision support. For example, tenet 1 requires that the minimum support that may be provided is one unit in a direct support role. Tenet 3 leads to the constraints that exist between phases.

8.3 The approach adopted

8.3.1 Overview of the approach

The OFC decision support aid was designed and prototyped using the standard ART/LISP AI environment available within the company because of the advantages of multiple knowledge representation schemes, incremental compilation, and interactive logical debugging. However, at every stage of the design, the final destination of the system was carefully considered, to prevent any combinatorial explosions which might have prevented a successful implementation in the constrained destination environment. Further checks were provided by calculations to establish the likely computing demands placed upon the delivery environment.

The actual implementation was achieved in three stages, the prototype, the first delivery version, written in Borland Turbo C and the final delivery version in full-blown Ada. The design and implementation is summarized in Fig. 8.4.

The process of development and implementation will be considered in four stages: knowledge elicitation, prototype development, first implementation and second implementation.

Tenet 1 : The organization must provide adequate field artillery support

Tenet 2 : The organization must weigh the main attack in offence, or most vulnerable area in defence

Tenet 3 : The organization must facilitate future operations

Tenet 4 : The organization must provide maximum feasible centralized control

Tenet 5 : The organization must provide immediately available field artillery support for the commander to influence the action

Tab. 8.1 Basic tenets of OFC.

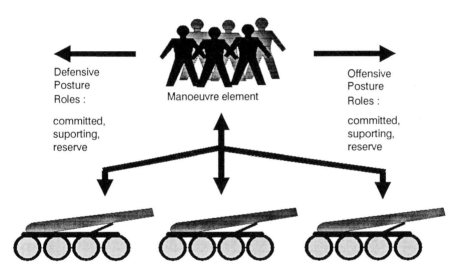

Defensive Posture Roles :

committed, suporting, reserve

Manoeuvre element

Offensive Posture Roles :

committed, suporting, reserve

Field artillery units each have a mission of type direct support, reinforcing, general support reinforcing or general support

OFC is a matching problem concerned with matching artillery elements to manoeuvre elements. Each manoeuvre element may have more than one artillery element associated with it.

Fig. 8.4 Elements to be matched in OFC.

8.3.2 Knowledge elicitation

For the purposes of knowledge elicitation, the military field manuals although fundamentally important, were found to be vague, out of date and often too general to be of much assistance. Three further sources were employed for knowledge elicitation. The company employs retired military personnel within its own ranks. They were consulted in the first instance. Their knowledge was brought up to date by a serving officer with eighteen years experience of the problem. Finally, with his help, a questionnaire was designed to gather knowledge from a wider range of personnel.

The man-machine interfacewas not developed as part of the AI prototype, although some work was carried out using storyboards and representations of the interface. The delivery version included the fully developed interface.

8.3.2 Development of the prototype

The prototype was developed using the viewpoint facility of ART, which corresponds to the 'worlds' facility in KEE. This facility allows the developer to spawn hypothetical organizations. Each single phase organization found to be feasible was then combined into a multi-phase solution. Many further solutions were eliminated using rules governing the constraints between phases.

Initial work produced a system where very often no hypotheses survived, due to the system over-constraining the problem. A system for incrementally relaxing the constraints was introduced allowing relaxation until one or more hypotheses survived.

The prototype proved that the concept behind the system was feasible. The system produced answers in about ten seconds or just less. Use was made of validation tools within ART to compare the resulting hypotheses with human expert judgement. One of the most helpful features of ART was that it allowed the behaviour of the system to be observed. In particular it was noticed that certain rules fired frequently, and others rarely. From these observations, it was possible to derive a deterministic algorithm. This would not have been possible without the development and observation of the prototype within ART. It represents the extension of the knowledge elicitation process through the use of prototyping. This enabled an order of magnitude performance improvement to be achieved in later versions.

8.3.3 First implementation

Using the knowledge gained from the prototyping in ART, it proved possible to map the reasoning process in ART onto a generate and test algorithm in C. The C implementation did not make use of those C facilities which could not be easily ported to Ada such as pointers to functions. This implementation reached conclusions in less than one second.

A further problem emerged at this stage, in the particular case where there are many 'correct' solutions. The human experts refused to accept that these situations were exactly equivalent and wanted the system to produce all possible solutions for

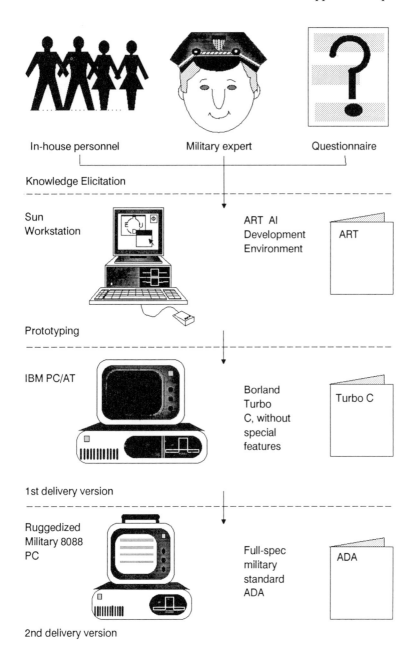

In-house personnel   Military expert   Questionnaire

Knowledge Elicitation

Sun
Workstation

ART AI
Development
Environment

ART

Prototyping

IBM PC/AT

Borland
Turbo
C, without
special
features

Turbo C

1st delivery version

Ruggedized
Military 8088
PC

Full-spec
military
standard
ADA

ADA

2nd delivery version

Fig. 8.5 The overall development process.

human evaluation. This required the incorporation of audit trails, to allow the stopping and starting of searches at will. Further adaptation, allowing user violation of single rules, permitted the use of the decision aid for simulation and training.

The largest remaining limitation of the system is the difficulty of maintaining the rule base. To modify or add rules, the user must have a knowledge of both C and the internal structures of the OFC decision support aid. Logical debugging, available under ART, is not possible, and the source code debugger is now the only available debugging tool.

The man-machine interfaceis based upon an in-house window package which provides a consistent graphical interfaceacross all the company's systems, on platforms from the Macintosh to military PC hardware. It is interesting to note that many people are impressed by the interface, and as a consequence, make the assumption that the system cannot be based upon AI technology. A classic illustration of the inherent prejudices which are unfortunately too often based upon fact.

8.3.4 Second implementation

From the C version, the final system written in Ada was derived. The system runs on a 4Mhz 8086 military terminal. It fulfills all the requirements of a military system whilst retaining many of the facilities of the AI prototype version. The development of the OFC system if repeated elsewhere would go a long way to addressing many of the prejudices remaining amongst software engineers.

8.4 Lessons to be learnt from the OFC experience

This work has shown that expert systems can be designed in such a way that the end system fulfills many of the traditional expectations of information systems:

(a) *Conformance to external standards.* The system conforms to the US DoD specifications for the Ada language and runs on standard ruggedized military hardware. This gives users, who may be sceptical about AI systems, confidence in the system. This will become increasingly important as more and stiffer standards are imposed by clients on the software developer.

(b) *Graphical user interface.* Part of the process of the transition from prototype to delivery version is the provision of a graphical user interface. This together with a wider consideration of human issues, for example, consideration of uses in training and simulation, is crucial to user acceptance of the system.

(c) *Efficient performance.* The performance of the delivery vehicle is within the one second response time required by the system. This is crucial in the usefulness of the system. Two things may be noted about performance. First, careful consideration was required at all times to prevent combinatorial explosion leading to poor response time. Secondly, in moving away from the

AI environment and structure, an order of magnitude improvement in performance was achieved, in spite of a move to less powerful hardware.

(d) Compatibility with basic hardware. There are many situations where traditional AI hardware will not be available, because of the environment, or simply because of cost. This system has shown how a system may be implemented on very basic hardware, without many of the compromises inherent in the 'shells' traditionally associated with small microcomputers and PCs.

This case study is notable because of the number of sacred cows from the expert systems field that it confounds. The work is characterized by a healthy pragmatism which if more widely adopted, will assist in the wider acceptance of expert systems as serious IT solutions.

8.5 Further reading

The work described in this chapter is presented in the following paper:
Dunkelberger, K.A. (1989) OFC: a deliverable military planning aid, *Applications of artificial intelligence* **VII, 725-734, SPIE vol1095.**

If the reader is interested further, it is suggested that they contact SPIE at
SPIE, P.O. Box 10, Bellingham WA USA 98227-0010,
or Dr Dunkelberger at
DACE, Magnavox Electronic Systems Co. 1313, Production Rd., Fort Wayne, Indiana 46808.

Case Study III: PAYE: An expert database system

This chapter is concerned with the integration of expert systems with database management systems (DBMS). The chapter starts with a consideration of this type of system. This is followed by a specific example. The example considered is an expert system for the determination of tax problems, called PAYE, written in PROLOG, integrated with a DBMS, written in Ingres. The system uses UNIX and C to provide an interface between the systems.

9.1 Expert database systems

The most common application of computers in commercial information processing is the database management system. Traditionally, they have been written in COBOL and run on mainframe computers. These computers require careful handling and clean environments and power supplies to provide good results. Recently, however, as computers have become more efficient, many applications formerly running on mainframes are able to make use of minicomputers. Many of these applications are written in 4GLs, which offer greater productivity to the system developer.

Typically, such applications run under the UNIX operating system, which offers flexibility for communication and integration. This provides the opportunity for interfacing a DBMS with an expert system. Torsun and Ng (1989) suggest a number of advantages which may arise from such integration:

- Expansion of the power and flexibility of a DBMS by the inclusion of an inference mechanism.
- Provision of complex operations for data manipulation, beyond the scope of current DBMS.
- Acceptability by users who are unfamiliar with programming concepts.
- Provision of a large number of facts for the expert system.
- Provision of multi-user facilities for expert systems.

These facilities may be viewed as the use of an expert system as an enhanced interface between the database and the user (Fig. 9.1). The extra system provides a more flexible interface, expanding both the scope of the system and the range of users. In this sense, it represents an 'intelligent' interface. The specific example we shall consider as a case study is a system devised at Bradford University for the

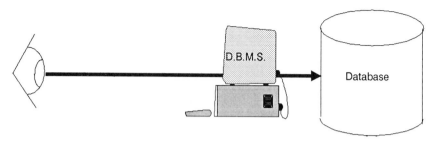

Database management system

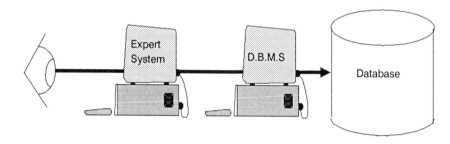

Integrated expert database system

Fig. 9.1 An expert system as interface.

problem domain of income tax. The work is published in detail in two papers (Torsun, 1987, and Torsun and Ng, 1989).

9.2 The problem

The system has been devised to provide guidance on personal taxation. The scope of the system includes Pay-as-you-earn (PAYE), National Insurance contributions (NIC) and statutory sick pay (SSP). The regulations concerning these schemes which form the basis of the knowledge to be encapsulated within the system are made up of UK Government Acts of Parliament, guidelines and pamphlets. The domain appears an attractive one, the knowledge being made up of rules and facts, which would appear to be ready-made for knowledge representation, particularly in PROLOG. However, on closer examination, the rules are found to be ambiguous, ill-defined, incomplete and self-contradictory. Further, and particularly important to the long-term effectiveness of the solution, they are subject to constant change as Government legislation requires updates, modifications and deletions.

The tax-rules themselves combine many different types of reasoning. Apart from rule-based reasoning, they derive from case-studies. For example, where an ambiguity exists in the rules, it is often resolved by a legal test-case. This must be incorporated into the knowledge base. Use is also made of analogical reasoning and hypothetical reasoning. The system must take account of time in its reasoning.

The aim of the system is to provide guidance for employers and tax officials in cases where expert guidance is required. An effective explanation facility is, therefore, important.

9.3 The solution

The overall system is summarized in Figure 9.2. We shall consider each component in detail.

9.3.1 The expert system component

The expert system component is written in PROLOG. For the purposes of integration, the PROLOG used is NIP Prolog (NIP Prolog, 1985), since this is written in C, and allows for a flexible and relatively efficient interface to C. The knowledge is represented in rules and facts, comprising some 2000 rules and 500 facts.

The knowledge is represented as PROLOG facts and rules. A typical rule from the system will have between 8 and 10 conditions and 1 to 6 actions. An example rule is shown in Tab. 9.1, with its PROLOG equivalent in Tab. 9.2.

The rules were derived from an analysis of the documentation concerning tax regulations. Ambiguities regarding court decisions and other areas were resolved by consultation with tax experts from the Inland Revenue.

A high priority was placed upon ease of modification of the knowledge base as a consequence of the transient nature of the problem domain. This was achieved by a top-down design strategy leading to a hierarchical structure for the system. The basic architecture is shown in Fig. 9.3, although only one area (Pay) is expanded.

Another priority is the user interface. The user is led through a simple interactive session providing the answer to simple questions through numerical menus, as illustrated in Tab. 9.3.

The conclusions are presented as a series of statements (Tab. 9.4).

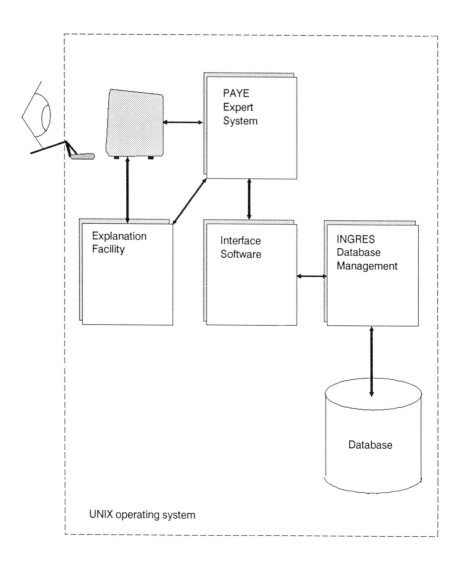

Fig. 9.2 The PAYE expert system.

IF employee is new employee
AND employee is school leaver
AND certificate A of form P46 is completed
AND pay > threshold
AND form P45 not produced
AND employment > 1 week

THEN

enter code for emergency use (200L) on deduction working sheet
AND set cumulative previous week's pay to nil
AND set cumulative previous week's tax to nil
AND send form P46 to tax office
AND calculate tax on cumulative basis using tables A and B
AND issue a coding claim from P15 to employee

Tab. 9.1 Sample tax rule.

new-employee (E) :-
new(E),
has-employee(E,P45),
school-leaver(E),
completed(E,certificate-A),
pay(E,PAY), threshold(THRESHOLD), PAY > THRESHOLD,
employment(E,WEEK), WEEK 1,
dws-tax-code(E,200L),
cumulative-prev-pay(E,0),
culmulative(E,TAX),
issue-form(E,P15).

Tab. 9.2 PROLOG representation of tax rules.

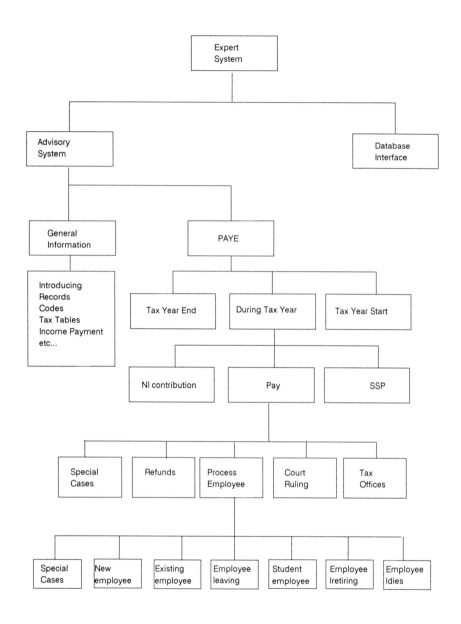

Fig. 9.3 Hierarchical structure of PAYE system.

Please choose the relevant area :

START OF TAX YEAR (BEFORE APRIL 6TH) 1

DURING THE TAX YEAR.. 2

END OF YEAR RETURNS 3

to return to main menu... 9

ITEM ? 2.

DURING TAX YEAR :

NEW EMPLOYEE... 1

SCHOOL LEAVER 2

EXISTING EMPLOYEE..3

LEAVING/LEFT..4

RETIRING/RETIRED...5

DIED IN EMPLOYMENT...6

REFUNDS...7

TAX OFFICE...8

to return to main menu...9

ITEM ? 4

Tab.9.3 Sample interactive session. (after Torsun)

MY CONCLUSION IS :

1. PREPARE EMPLOYEE "green.ic" DEDUCTION WORKING SHEET (dws)

2. ENTER TAX CODE 320H ON DWS FOR EMPLOYEE "green.ic"

3. CALCULATE TAX ON A WEEKLY BASIS

4. ENTER ON TOP OF PART 3 OF FORM P45

PENSION 0 WEEK 1 BASIS

5. DO NOT COMPLETE FORM P45.

Tab.9.4 Sample PAYE conclusions. (after Torsun)

The explanation facility for the system is based upon a rule tracing facility. The user may request explanation through one of four commands:

Why? why a particular piece of information is asked for or a piece of advice given.
How? How a particular piece of advice is arrived at.
Whynot? Why a particular decision cannot be made.
Explain? Gives explanation of specific items requested e.g. tax codes in the form of English text.

The performance of the system was judged to be comparable to human experts. However, the investment required to reach this level of performance was considerable.

9.3.2 The database management system component

The database management functions are handled by Ingres (Stonebraker, Wong and Krep, 1986), a relational database management system. Ingres is attractive because it runs under UNIX and may be accessed in one of two ways. The database may be interrogated interactively through the query language QUEL. Alternatively, the embedded QUEL (EQUEL) facility may be used to allow the database to be manipulated by means of a C program. Through the use of C commands, the database may communicate with the interface and through the interface to the expert system itself. The manipulation of the database from the expert system will be considered in the next section.

9.3.3 The TCEDI interface

The interface is of the tightly-coupled type discussed in Chapter 5. A number of objectives were set for the interface at the outset.

- Efficiency is very important, particularly where large amounts of data are to be moved.
- The interface should be flexible to changes in either the expert system or DBMS.
- The interface should be transparent to the user, with no knowledge of the underlying query language required.
- The interface should be neutral, not imposing restrictions upon either system.
- The interface should be easy to maintain.

The interface makes use of the fact that both implementation media, Ingres and NIP Prolog are written in C and will communicate with C. In effect, the interface is made up of two interfaces: PROLOG to C, C to Ingres. This is shown schematically in Fig. 9.4, together with the practical realization where the C to Ingres interface is made up of three phases.

The interactions between PROLOG and Ingres may occur at one of three levels, system level operations, relation level operations and record level operations.

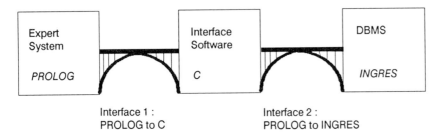

TCEDI : A schematic view

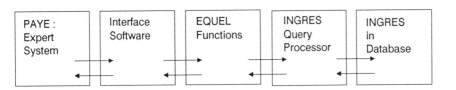

TCEDI : the practical realization

Fig. 9.4 Structure of the TCEDI interface.

System level operations are necessary where multiple databases are used. Examples of such operations are

'create new database',   implemented as i_creatdb(Database-Name),
'start up database',   implemented as i_ingres(Database_Name),
'exit current database', implemented as i_exit.

Relation level operations act upon a relation rather than a whole database, e.g.

'create new relation' implemented as   i_create(Reln,
[Atn1,Format1,Length1], [Atn2,Format2,Length2],

[Atni,Formati,Lengthi])

where Reln is the name of the new relation,
and   Atni is the attribute name,
and   Formati is the attribute format,
and   Lengthi is the attribute length.

The final type of operation occurs at the record level acting upon individual database records, e.g.

to append a new record,
i_append(Reln,[[Atn1,Atv1],[,]....[Atni,Atvi]]);
where Atni and Atvi are the attribute name and value respectively.

9.4 Conclusions

The resulting integrated solution realises many of the objectives set out for the project. An efficient interface is established between the expert and database components. Inevitably, there is an overhead in any interfaced discrete system associated with the communication of data between components. In the next chapter we shall compare the approach adopted to some of the alternatives.

The system also shows that the principles of structured analysis and design leading to a maintainable and adaptable solution can be applied to at least some expert system projects.

Finally, the system shows that expert systems may be integrated to good effect with large scale databases, and that where such applications have been written in a system such as Ingres, running under UNIX, such integration may be added retrospectively without the loss of integrity associated with loosely-coupled systems.

9.5 Further Reading

These two papers describe the PAYE system and the TCEDI interface in detail:

Torsun, I. S. (1987) PAYE: A tax expert system, *Research and Development in Expert Systems* **III**, *Proceedings ES'86,* 69-80, C.U.P.

Torsun,I. S and Ng. Y. M. (1989) TCEDI: Tightly-coupled expert database system interface, *Research and Development in Expert Systems* **V**, *Proceedings ES'88,* 210-223, C.U.P.

The 1987 paper deals with the PAYE expert system in detail. The 1989 paper describes how the authors developed the TCEDI interface to link the expert system to the DBMS. The second paper also contains a survey of the methods available for integration.

CHAPTER TEN

Strategies for integrated system design

The whole of the book thus far has been aimed at raising the issue of the integration of expert systems into mainstream software. If it has succeeded in raising the issue to the level where the reader is interested in applying the ideas to their own environment, then the time has come to suggest how this may be done.

Conventional wisdom might suggest a rigid methodology as the way forward. A methodology will be presented, but hopefully it is not too rigid. It is presented alongside two other approaches, together with some guidance as to which may best be adopted. This section will be most successful, however, if it stimulates the reader to develop their own approach based upon those presented here.

10.1 Strategies for integration

Integration of expert systems is carried out by different people in various situations for a variety of reasons. It, therefore, seems unreasonable to suggest that there is a single strategy for designing integrated systems. After all, we have already seen that there are different ISD methodologies available to the information system designer and that each has its own characteristics which affect its suitability to any particular problem. Thus the starting point for integrated system design is the question,

'Why do I want an integrated expert system?'

If the answer to this question lies in the inadequacy of existing single technologies then an integrated solution is worth investigating. These inadequacies may be in a number of areas, such as lack of traditional software virtues, lack of conformity to standards, or more simply the inability of a single technology to model the problem and provide an effective solution.

If the answer to this basic question lies elsewhere then the project should be scrutinized carefully. Expert systems designed for their own sake or to prove the cleverness of the designer or the technology have not provided effective solutions in the past. Integration for its own sake is unlikely to fare any better.

Three strategies will be presented here. In choosing between them, the potential system designer should bear in mind two things. The first consideration is the system that the designer would build if confined to a single technology. The second is the type of benefit that is anticipated from adopting that particular strategy. The reader is advised to match their needs to Fig. 10.1.

If the system has been conceived as an information system in the first instance based upon algorithmic solutions, and if the benefits sought from integration are

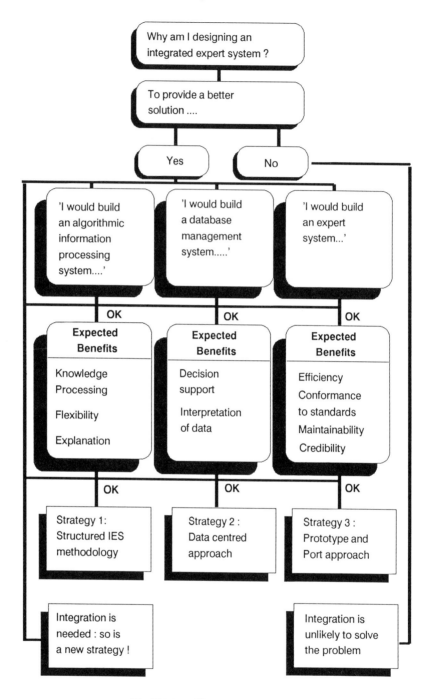

Fig. 10.1 Matching strategies to needs.

greater flexibility and the ability to handle problems in terms of knowledge and symbolic reasoning, then strategy 1, the structured IES methodology is suggested. Alternatively, if the system starts life as a database management system, and greater decision support and interpretation of data is required, then strategy 2, the data-centred approach, leading to an expert database system is likely to prove more effective. Finally, if what you really want is an expert system but a traditional stand-alone system is unacceptable because of quality considerations, external standards or simple prejudice, then strategy 3 is your best bet. If existing technologies alone cannot solve your problem, but none of the above describes your problem, then turn to the section at the end of the chapter, entitled 'Other strategies for integration'.

10.2 Strategy 1: structured integrated expert system (IES) methodology

The starting point for this methodology is the traditional waterfall lifecycle, as described in Chapter 4. To briefly summarize, five phases are considered:

(a) *Requirements analysis. The aims, objectives and limits of the system are established in consultation with the client. They must be defined in a way that is understandable to the client and detailed enough for development staff.*

(b) *System and Software Design. The requirements are used to allocate tasks as either hardware or software systems. Software design is concerned with transforming the software requirements into a form suitable for representation as a program.*

(c) *Implementation and Unit Testing. This section is concerned with coding, and ensuring each unit of code meets the specification.*

(d) *System Testing. The units are combined to form a whole system, and the completed system is tested to ensure that it performs according to specification.*

(e) *Operation and Maintenance.* The product is installed and used by the client. Maintenance is ongoing, concerned not just with 'bug-fixes' but improving the product and answering new user requirements as they emerge.

The problems of employing methodologies based upon this approach in the development of integrated expert systems have already been highlighted. In particular they lie in the areas of requirements analysis, task allocation within the integrated scenario, the design and implementation of knowledge based modules, and in combining the modules back into a whole.

The structured IES methodology for integrated system design attempts to address these issues, whilst retaining some of the features of the waterfall model. The methodology is shown in Fig. 10.2. The stages of the development lifecycle are described in detail below.

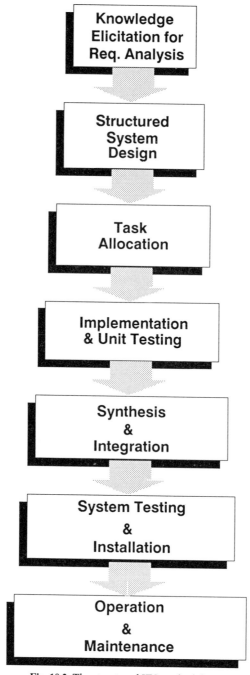

Fig. 10.2 The structured IES methodology.

10.2.1 Knowledge elicitation for requirements analysis

The failure of existing requirements analysis procedures in the design of expert systems because of the ill-defined nature of the problems under investigation has led to the development of RUDE-based approaches. This framework sets out to limit the iterative cycle to the requirements analysis, facilitating the refinement of the requirements specification, but permitting the development of well-structured maintainable software. The aims of this phase are fourfold.

- To facilitate the transfer of knowledge from domain expert to the system developers.
- To improve communication to facilitate expert feedback
- To establish a correct level of expertise for the intended user.
- To establish the scale of the problem.

The process seeks to alleviate some of the major bottlenecks in the development of expert systems, specifically, communication between the knowledge engineer and the domain expert, a lack of user modelling and the scaling problem.

From the feasibility study, the knowledge engineer can go to the domain expert for an initial knowledge elicitation session. From this he can draw up an initial specification for the system. This specification must include the functions required by the system together with a preliminary user model and an analysis of the depth of the model required by the system to provide meaningful results

This initial specification forms the basis for further sessions with the domain expert, to gauge reaction and to ensure that the knowledge engineer fully understands the implications of the problem. In addition, the user model and a prototype interface should be tested on a typical intended user. This process should be repeated until three conditions are satisfied, each derived from one of the three principal stakeholders in the system development. The domain expert must be satisfied that the true depth of the problem has been grasped, whilst the intended user should express satisfaction with the intended user interfaceand confidence in their intended role. Finally, the knowledge engineer should reach the point where they are confident that his own level of understanding is sufficient.

At this stage, the specification may be documented to include the elements listed above. The final documented specification is not written in stone, but should only be changed beyond this point by mutual agreement of all interested parties. It is inevitable in the development of a system of this type that changes will need to be made later in the lifecycle. They should be minimized and be agreed by consensus to avoid upsetting the balance agreed at the requirements stage.

10.2.2 Structuring and software design (SSD).

In this framework, this stage is required to produce a modular structure for the system, sufficiently detailed to allow the task allocation to be carried out. The problem must be divided up into tasks suitable for allocation. A reductionist strategy may be adopted, and the structured analysis methodology of DeMarco (1979) is suitable for the purpose. Experience from expert systems has shown that this reductionist approach may not be easily accepted by experts, from whom a knowledge of the problem may be gleaned. This may due to very real problems in analysis, or due to a reluctance to dissect their own expertise.

In conventional knowledge engineering, it is this stage that often forms a bottleneck. The demands made by this approach are not as great as in conventional knowledge engineering, since it is unnecessary to break down each task to the elemental level which may be represented by rules or frames or other knowledge representation scheme. Here the SSD analysis is required only to elucidate a level of detail sufficient to identify individual tasks. The output from this stage may either be in pseudocode or diagrammatic form.

The results of the SSD phase will be first a data flow diagram, then a structure chart. This type of analysis was used in Case Study I for the fringe pattern analysis application and the resulting structure chart is shown in Fig. 10.3. From such a structure chart, a high level pseudocode representation may be derived (Tab. 10.1).

Once such a task analysis is carried out, it is necessary to assign the tasks to the most appropriate agency: human, machine as knowledge processor, and machine as information processor.

10.2.3 Task allocation

At this stage, each task may be viewed as a module in a notional modular piece of software. The allocation of tasks is influenced by the strengths and weaknesses of each agency outlined in Chapter 5, where the task allocation process has been described in greater detail, and illustrated in Fig. 5.8.

Within the structured IES methodology, the task allocation process is designed to assign each task identified by the system and software design phase. The results may then be represented diagrammatically, as in Fig. 10.4 or as annotations to the pseudocode (Tabs. 10.2 and 10.3).

There is a degree of iteration built in to the methodology at this point. When task allocation is considered, some tasks designated under structured analysis may be found to be compound tasks, that is, they need to be tackled by more than one technology. These should be replaced by their elemental tasks in an extension of the structuring and system design phase, before task allocation is carried out. Thus, if the underlying structure in Fig. 10.4 is compared to the structure in Fig. 10.3, further simplification is seen to have taken place.

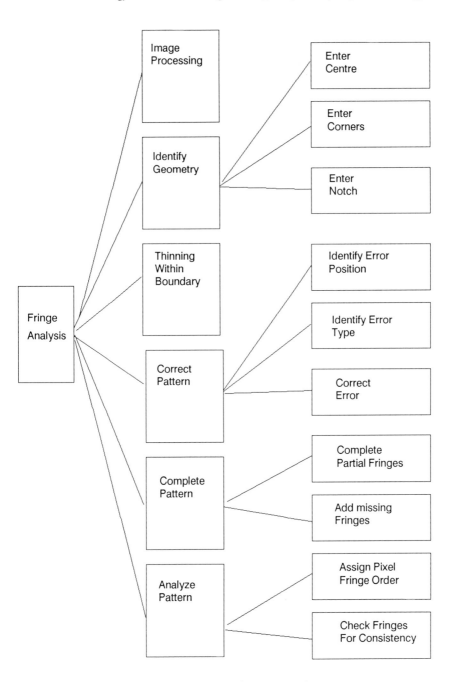

Fig. 10.3 Structure chart from Case Study I.

```
PROGRAM Fringe Analysis ;
PROCEDURE ImageProcessing ;
PROCEDURE IdentifyGeometry ;
BEGIN
EnterCentre ;
EnterCorners ;
EnterNotch ;
END ;
PROCEDURE ThinningWithinBoundary ;
PROCEDURE CorrectPattern ;
BEGIN
IdentifyErrorPosition ;
IdentifyErrorType ;
CorrectError ;
END ;
PROCEDURE CompletePattern ;
BEGIN
CompletePartialFringes ;
AddMissingFringes ;
END ;
PROCEDURE AnalyzePattern ;
BEGIN
AssignPixelFringeOrder ;
CheckFringesConsistent ;
END ;

BEGIN
ImageProcessing ;
IdentifyGeometry ;
ThinningWithinBoundary ;
CorrectPattern ;
CompletePattern ;
AnalyzePattern ;
END.
```

Tab 10.1 Pseudo-code output from SSD phase.

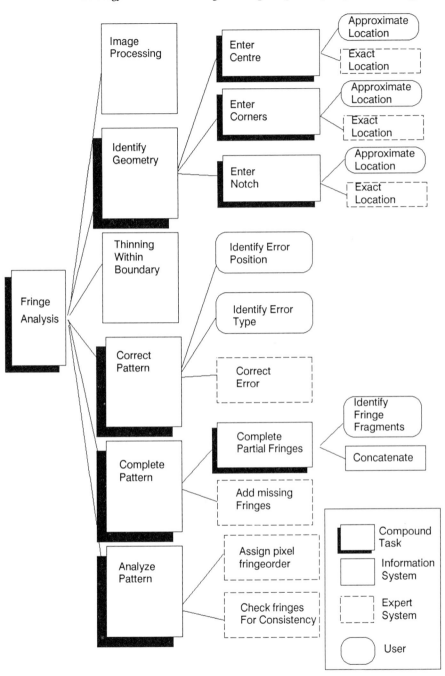

Fig. 10.4 Output from task allocation.

```
PROGRAM FringeAnalysis ;

PROCEDURE EnterCentre ;
BEGIN
ApproximateLocation ; {user}
ExactLocation ; {information}
END ;
PROCEDURE EnterCorners ;
BEGIN
ApproximateLocation ; {user}
ExactLocation ; {information}
END ;
PROCEDURE EnterNotch ;
BEGIN
ApproximateLocation ; {user}
ExactLocation ; {information}
END ;
PROCEDURE IdentifyErrorPosition ; {user}

PROCEDURE IdentifyErrorType ; {user}

PROCEDURE CorrectError {Knowledge}

PROCEDURE CompletePartialFringes ;
BEGIN
IdentifyFringeFragments ; {user}
Concatenate ; {Knowledge}
END ;

PROCEDURE AddMissingFringes ; {Knowledge}

PROCEDURE AssignFringeOrderToPixels ; {Knowledge}

PROCEDURE CheckFringesForConsistency ; {Knowledge}
```

Tab 10.2 Annotated pseudo-code after allocation.

```
PROCEDURE ImageProcessing ; {Information}
PROCEDURE IdentifyGeometry ;
BEGIN
EnterCentre ;
EnterCorners ;
EnterNotch ;
END ;
PROCEDURE ThinningWithinBoundary ; {Information}

PROCEDURE CorrectPattern ;
BEGIN
IdentifyErrorPosition ; {user}
IdentifyErrorType ;{user}
CorrectError ;{Knowledge}
END ;
PROCEDURE CompletePattern ;
BEGIN
CompletePartialFringes ;
AddMissingFringes ;
END ;
PROCEDURE AnalyzePattern ;
BEGIN
AssignPixelFringeOrder ;
CheckFringesConsistent ;
END ;

BEGIN
ImageProcessing ;
IdentifyGeometry ;
ThinningWithinBoundary ;
CorrectPattern ;
CompletePattern ;
AnalyzePattern.
END.
```

Tab. 10.3 Annotated peudo-code (continued).

10.2.4 Implementation and unit testing

Once each task is allocated, the corresponding module may be tackled using conventional methods or tools if they are available.

The information processing modules may be designed as conventional structured code, typically in a language such as C or Pascal. If a CASE tool is employed for the structuring and system design phase then this may be employed to assist in the coding of the information modules.

The design of the knowledge-based modules will depend upon the demands placed upon them. The starting point for design is the representation of a the module concerned in some sort of AI environment such as an AI toolkit or perhaps a declarative language such as PROLOG or some of the more adequate PC based shells. A prototype system is then derived which may be integrated with the rest of the system in a number of ways.

Ideally, for the sake of simplicity and integrity, the derivation and implementation of the prototype system will result in a portable data structure. We have shown in earlier chapters how AI data structures may be represented in 3GLs such as Pascal. Within the confines of a 3GL, the options of conversion or construction are open to the designer.

Conversion can be used where exploration of the prototype reveals that it is possible to implement much or all of the knowledge-based module using an algorithmic approach together with the limited logical constructs available such as IF..THEN or CASE...OF. The limitation here is set by what it is possible to represent in this way.

Construction is the use of predefined data structures constructed in a 3GL. This is often how expert system shells work in practice. The limitation here is set by the complexity and cost of this approach. In practice, there is a tradeoff here between the usefulness of specific data structures and the economy of reusable libraries of predefined general purpose structures. The shell in many cases represents an economical solution because of its general purpose nature, but can also prove to be ineffectual in consequence. This approach is more practicable for the construction of knowledge-based modules than for whole expert systems, because the complexity of single modules can be much less.

Failing this, the use of a hybrid language may be considered, such as C++ or object-oriented dialects of Pascal. These languages allow the developer more flexibility in their data structures, particularly in the use of frames to represent knowledge. C++ offers three major enhancements over C, which are helpful to the integrated system designer:

- data abstractions,
- support for object-oriented design and programming, and
- improvements to some existing C constructs.

If this still does not provide enough flexibility, the developer is recommended to develop the knowledge based module within a dialect of Prolog, preferably one which is designed to interface to a 3GL. This type of PROLOG is now available for the PC. For example, modules implemented in Turbo Prolog can be called from Turbo C, allowing the user to develop the information-based components in C, whilst integrating the knowledge-based modules by calling the Prolog code from a main program written in C. Dialects of PROLOG are also available for graphical workstation such as the SUN, and machine such as the Apple Macintosh.

The choice of implementation medium, procedural language, such as C or Pascal, hybrid language such as C + + or Object Pascal, or declarative language such as PROLOG will depend upon the demands made by the knowledge-based modules. The golden rule is that the simplest solution that is effective will produce the optimum solution. The merits of each are summarized in Tab. 10.4.

Language Type	Example	AI structures represented	Integration to information and user modules
Procedural (3GL) Language	C Pascal Fortran	Simple rules Others using complex constructs	Straightforward
Hybrid 3GL with object oriented extensions	C + + Object Pascal Turbo Pascal (v5.5)	As above, plus frames	Restricted to 'parent' language
Declarative Language	PROLOG	Facts, Rules, Semantic networks, Frames	Implementation dependent, but more complex in all cases

Tab. 10.4 Methods for implementing KBS modules.

The user modules will require careful interface design, with a degree of user testing to ensure that the perceived user model is appropriate. The user interfacemay be implemented in the same medium as the rest of the system or using a proprietary interface development tool. The interface must be designed with the whole system in mind, presenting a uniform face to the outside world irrespective of the type module in operation at any one time. In particular, the interface must accommodate any explanation provided by knowledge-based

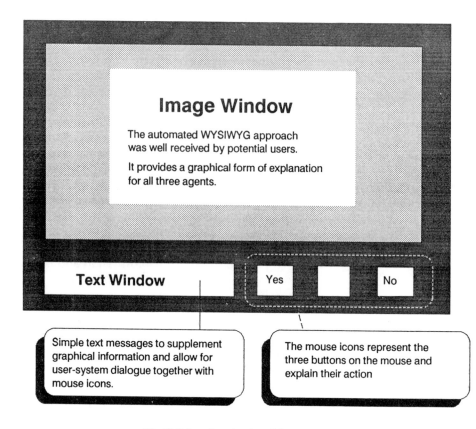

Fig. 10.5 Interface developed for case study I.

modules. The interface for the system in Case study I was designed with this in mind (Fig. 10.5).

The type of interface and the development tools available for implementation will vary enormously depending upon the hardware platform. This will affect substantially the approach to implementation of an interface. We shall consider three common types of hardware, PCs, graphical workstations and mainframes and consider the implications of each for interface design.

PC systems. The popularity of the PC continues to grow and with the availability of hardware based around the 80386 and 80486 chips together with expanded memory capabilities, their popularity for larger applications is likely to grow. Sophisticated interfaces are increasingly associated with PC applications and many of the PC software development environments, including those based around PROLOG, as well as C and Pascal are incorporating interface development toolboxes. This provides an efficient way to implement the interface, and minimises any integration problems.

Graphical Workstations. During the 1980s, the graphical workstation has become a very popular hardware platform, characterized by multitasking within a graphical environment, coupled with extensive computing power. In such cases, it is usual for the manufacturer to provide proprietary interfacing tools, often based upon the X Windows standard. Implementation of an interfaceshould not be too difficult using these tools, and integration to standard 3GLs, particularly C, should be readily available. However, integration to PROLOG or other languages may be more difficult.

Mainframes. Many applications still run on traditional mainframe computers. In such applications, interfaces are generally very crude and text-based. No special tools are likely to be available or of great value.

The key to a good implementation is the least complex method to realise the full implications of the interface design.

Unit testing should be carried out for each module. This restricts the complexity under test, and makes realistic testing possible. The system can then be assembled for system testing and integration

10.2.5 Synthesis and integration

The extent to which synthesis is an issue depends upon the homogeneity of the modules constructed in the previous phase. For example, if it is possible to construct the system in a uniform 3GL environment, using an integral interface implementation toolbox, then the integration aspect is no greater than for any other structured program. If however, the system incorporates modules in different languages or the use of proprietary interface implementation tools then special care is need to ensure system integrity.

PC applications are more likely to be implemented within a homogeneous environment. Larger applications, running on graphical workstations are more likely to require specific work to integrate components. Most of these applications will run under the UNIX operating system, and it is possible that the facilities of this system may be utilized, as in Case Study II. If UNIX is to utilized to any great extent, it is likely that the integration process will be simplified by the use of C or C++ or the implementation, because of the links available between the C language and the UNIX operating system.

10.2.6 System testing and installation

This does not differ a great deal from conventional systems, except that where substantial interfacing is required between information and knowledge processing, extra testing will be required to ensure that the synthesis and integration procedure has been effective. Acceptance testing is often skimped by system developers, but time spent in this way is a good investment against future maintenance costs.

10.2.7 Maintenance and operation

The resulting system should be a well-structured, well-tested piece of code. As such it should be maintainable and reliable. The only difference that may lead to problems is that adaptation of the system may be more difficult due to the extra complexity associated with the incorporation of the knowledge-based modules

The structured IES methodology is designed to allow the designer a degree of freedom, particularly in the implementation phase. This has been done for two reasons. The first is the vastly differing needs arising in different situations. The second is the belief that no single methodology can provide a 'correct' solution, and that rigid adherence to methodology can never replace human creativity, else we would have expert systems writing all our programmes.

The structured IES methodology is, therefore, proposed as a framework within which the system designer can work. The key areas are in the design phases, at structured system design and task allocation. If these phases are carried out successfully, then the correct decisions to be made about implementation will become apparent.

The author acknowledges that the approach makes use of tried and tested ideas, such as structured analysis. This is consistent with the underlying philosophy of making use of those techniques that produce effective solutions, rather than inventing new ones or making use of others for their own sake.

However, even with a certain in-built flexibility, the Structured IES methodology is not the best approach to all problems. Consider, as an alternative a data-centred approach.

10.3 Strategy 2: The data-centred approach

The data-centred approach is appropriate where a database management system (DBMS) is envisaged, but the designer would like extra facilities to sort and extract data. Many organizations are now facing serious problems in terms of an 'information overload'. By designing an expert system to run on top of the database, the data extracted may be first sorted by the computer, in order to present the user with more useful information.

This type of problem may be tackled using data-centred approach, illustrated in Fig. 10.6, contrasting with the other two strategies which may be regarded as 'code-centred'. The approach will be considered under the headings of design and implementation.

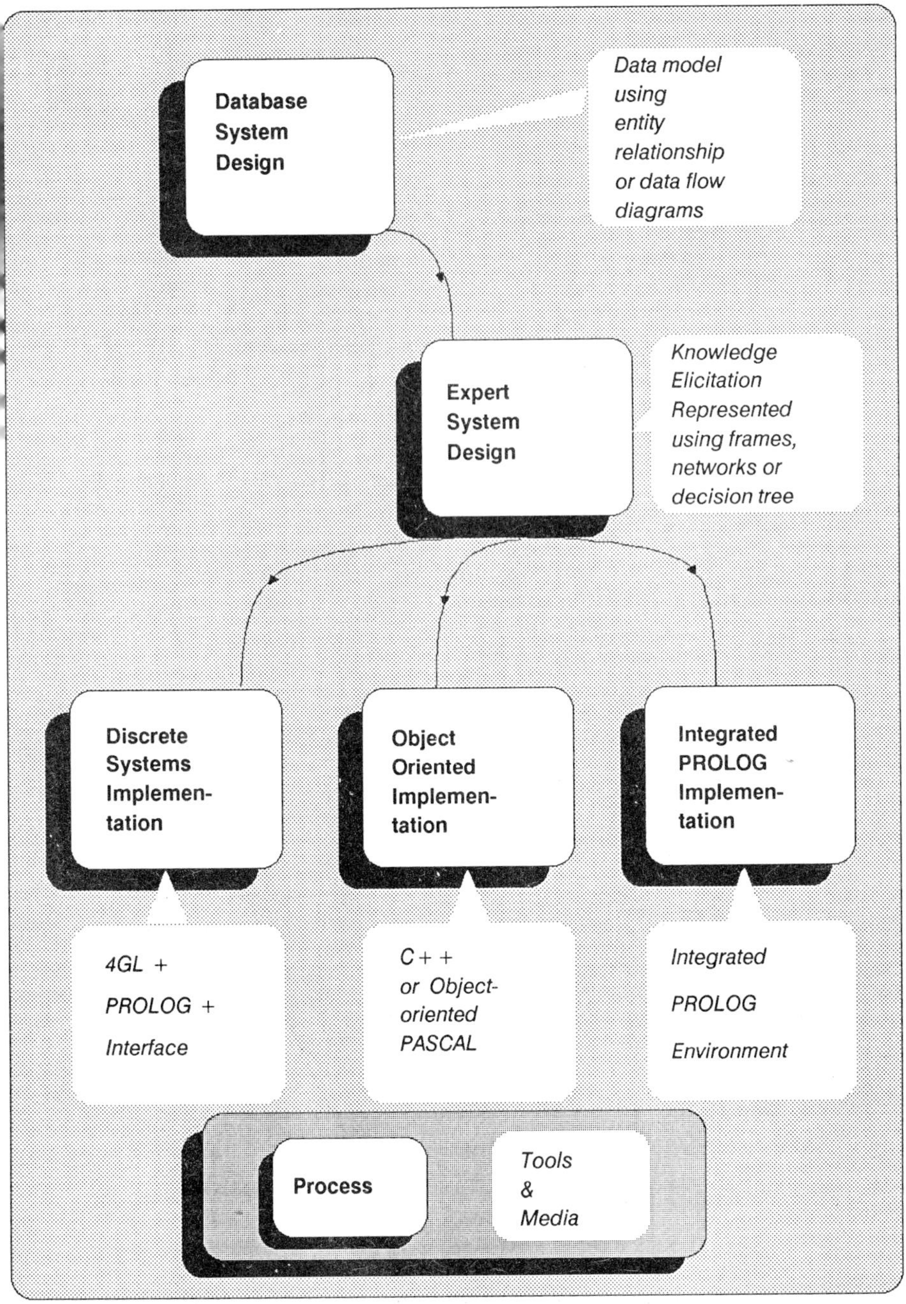

Database System Design

Data model using entity relationship or data flow diagrams

Expert System Design

Knowledge Elicitation Represented using frames, networks or decision tree

Discrete Systems Implementation

Object Oriented Implementation

Integrated PROLOG Implementation

4GL +

PROLOG +

Interface

C + +
or Object-oriented PASCAL

Integrated

PROLOG

Environment

Process

Tools & Media

Fig. 10.6 The data-centered approach.

10.3.1 Design

The design stage of the system is clearly divided into expert system design and database design. It may further emerge that a discrete interface is required, and this will also have to be considered.

The first design stage is the database, and the best approach here is one of the recognized methodologies for database design such as SSADM (Ashworth and Goodland, 1990) or IEM (described in Chapter 4). The design phases of these methodologies are based around the construction of a data model, typically an entity-relationship model. This may be constructed with the aid of a front-end CASE tool if one is available. Failing this, it may be constructed using a simple drawing package. A considerable user input is required at this stage as the developer is unlikely to fully appreciate the data needs of the problem. This involvement may be regarded as the first stage of the knowledge acquisition process for the project. Once the data model has been agreed with the user, it may be used as a starting point for knowledge elicitation for the expert system. A sample entity relationship model is shown in Figs. 10.7 and 10.8.

This is a simplified version of a model of the data structures required by a housing department in a local authority or a housing association. The key relationship in the diagram is the relationship between customer and dwelling unit, which may be a house or a flat or equivalent. Associated with the customer are ownership details, benefit details and records of any incidents. Associated with the dwelling unit are details of the type of property, its construction, amenities, maintenance and associated garages.

The knowledge required from the elicitation process is concerned with how the client makes use of the data in the database and what knowledge he uses in the process. Consider, for example, a housing manager. He is constantly under pressure to ensure that rent arrears are kept to a minimum. In a typical housing department, he may have ten thousand or more properties to manage. We could implement a knowledge-based procedure to monitor those customers who have gone into arrears.

The manager may have six levels of action available to him:

A pleasant reminder
A nasty letter
A visit from a housing officer
A threat to go to court
A summons to appear at court
An eviction order

Clearly, he is going to use these procedures increasingly sparingly as their severity increases. He uses his knowledge of people's actions and circumstances to make a decision. We may list some of the factors affecting his decision below:

'If the tenant is in arrears two weeks running and its getting worse then we would send a pleasant reminder'

'If it goes on getting worse for the next week, then we would send the nasty letter'

' If it starts to reduce over two weeks then we would start at the top again '

' If the letters don't work then I send a staff member round '

' If they find extenuating circumstances we agree a figure to pay off the arrears and then stop the arrears chasing procedure'

'If they are a bad payer then we short circuit the letters and send the officer round after two weeks'

'If they still don't pay after a visit and six weeks arrears, then we threaten to take them to court'.

'Two weeks after the threat to go to court the summons is sent'

'The final act is eviction - only used as a last resort'

Tab. 10.5 Knowledge about arrears collection.

Is the tenant in arrears?
Was the tenant in arrears last week?
Are the arrears getting worse?
Are there external factors?
Is the tenant a bad payer?

The system is going to have to monitor the answers to these questions over time, just as the manager would have to. A knowledge elicitation exercise might elicit some of the comments listed in Tab. 10.5.

From this, a decision tree may be derived (Fig. 10.9). If this was a stand alone expert system then the answers to the questions would come from the user. However, in this case, they may be drawn direct from the database.

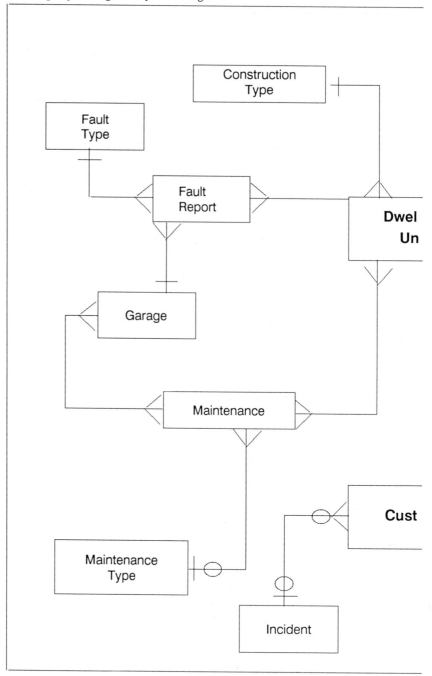

Fig. 10.7 Sample E-R diagram (1).

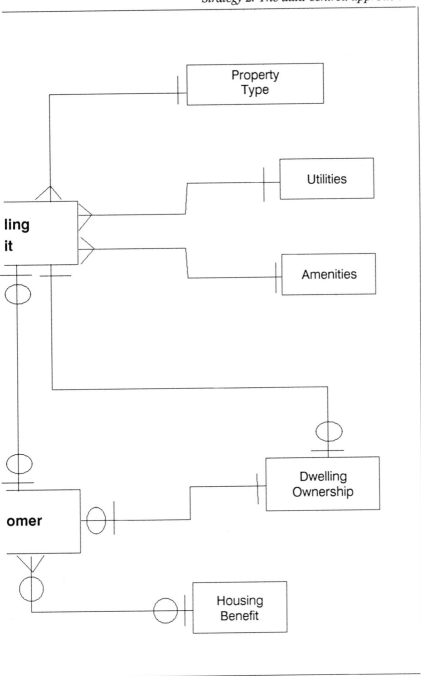

Fig. 10.8 Sample E-R diagram (2)

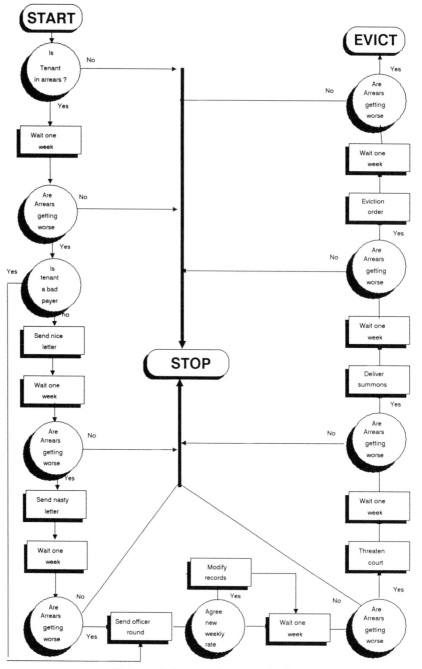

Fig. 10.9 Decision tree for arrears chasing.

The interface design will depend upon the choice of implementation media. In some cases, it will form part of the expert system or database system design, in others it will require separate implementation.

10.3.3 Implementation

The implementation procedure will depend upon the specific needs of the project. In a typical problem of this sort, the expert system component runs on top of the database management system, and therefore the implementation needs of the database management system (DBMS) will tend to dominate the implementation process. In such cases, the DBMS may be implemented in a 4GL, such as Ingres employed in case study III. The implemented database may be based upon the data model drawn up in the design phase. If the data model is successful, then the entities in the data model should translate readily into records in the implemented database. The use of code generators, such as those supplied with the IEF case tool, is not recommended as the resulting code is very difficult to interface to the expert system.

If this approach is adopted then the interface must be designed as a separate item to allow communication between the DBMS and the expert system. The resulting implementation will be two separate systems which are linked by data exchange. The expert system replaces the user input with automated input (Fig. 10.10).

Fig. 10.10 Expert system replaces database user.

This two-system implementation whilst not producing an integrated system ma provide the best solution. In applications where a large database is required, thi will almost certainly be true. However, the problem lies in maintaining integrit between the two systems. Any changes to one system will require correspondin, alterations to the other. The task of maintaining such a system is difficult. Th alternative is to look for a genuinely integrated solution. At least three possibilitie exist which may be explored.

In recent years, some of the database management tools such as Ingres hav introduced facilities for handling rules and objects within the databas environment itself. The latest version of the Ingres product boasts rule handling offering features such as forward chaining and recursion. It also offers facilities fo object manipulation, allowing the programmer to define their own datatypes functions and operators. These significant extensions will allow some exper system functionality to be built into the DBMS itself. This brings with it advantage of simplicity, integrity, efficiency and programmer productivity. If the systen developers can satisfy their needs with these facilities then this is an attractive implementation route. However, the facilities offered remain less flexible than a language such as PROLOG. In cases where the capabilities of the interna functions are exceeded, the developer must look elsewhere for implementatio media.

Object-oriented programming techniques are well-suited to combining bot knowledge and data records. Consider the following example, again from the housing management scenario. One of the largest headaches in housing management is the prioritization of repair and maintenance jobs. The following comments might be made by the housing manager in discussing the decision-making process to assign a priority varying from 1 (urgent..within 2 hours) to 5 (routine.. inside 3 months) to the job.

'The first priority has to be 'Is the situation life-threatening?''

'After life-threatening situations, the next priority are those repairs where dela might cause further problems.'

'Elderly and disabled tenants must get priority'

'Babies and young children are another priority'

'Minor repairs tend to get higher priority because they can be done quickly and reduce our backlog'

These comments may be summarized in terms of the following queries:
'Is the situation life-threatening?'
'Is the situation causing further deterioration of the property?'
'Does the repair affect basic, essential amenities?'

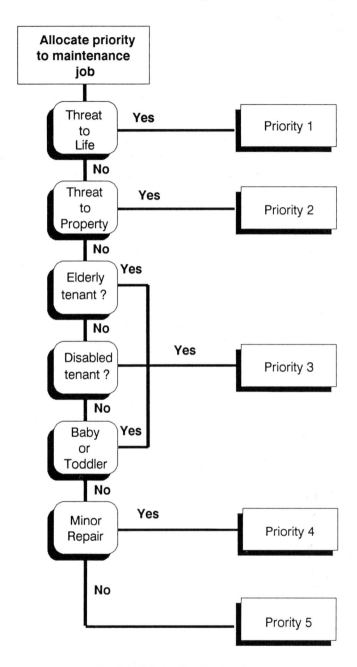

Fig.10.11 Priority allocation function.

'Is the tenant elderly?'
'Is the tenant disabled?'
'Are young children in the house?'
'Is it a minor repair?'

The knowledge expressed here may be represented in a decision tree (Fig. 10.11). The decision-making requires information about both the tenant and the property. The data required may be drawn from a database consisting of objects, implemented in C++ or object-oriented Pascal, with one object carrying information about the tenant and the other the repair. Fig. 10.12 illustrates these objects, highlighting the slots manipulated by the priority assignment function.

Object Title	Tenant	Object Title	Repair
Name	Smith	**Place**	Roof
D.O.B	21.06.16	**Repair Type**	Slate Replaced
Disabled	No		
Elderly	No	**Life Threat**	No
Children	2		
D.O.BChild	21.03.90	**Property Threat**	No
		Minor Repair	Yes

Fig. 10.12 Objects representing knowledge.

If constructed in an object-oriented dialect of Pascal, the object may be manipulated in a similar manner to a record. A sample of the code required to represent the decision-making process in Fig. 10.11 is shown in Tabs. 10.6 and 10.7. An object-oriented dialect of Pascal is used rather than C + +, because of its greater clarity.

Knowledge can be used not just to automate the data sorting process, but other functions such as data maintenance. For example, the date of birth of the tenant can be used to update automatically the slot 'elderly' when the tenant reaches a specific age. Similarly, the number of babies and toddlers may be monitored so that when the youngest reaches a particular age, the tenant no longer receives special treatment.

Object-oriented programming has not been widely accepted within the commercial community unlike fourth generation languages. However, the

```
{ DECLARATIONS }


TYPE
DateOfBirth : RECORD
day : 1..31 :
month : 1..12
year  : integer ;
END :
VAR
Tenant : object :
TenantDOB : DateOfBirth :
Name : string ;
Disabled : boolean :
Elderly : boolean :
Babies : integer ;
BabiesDOB : DateOfBirth :
END ;
```

Tab. 10.6 Object-oriented PASCAL source code.

```
Repair : object :
LifeThreatening : boolean ;
PropertyThreatening : boolean :
RepairDescription : string :
MinorRepair : boolean ;
END ;


Priority : 1..5 ;


PROCEDURE Assign Repair Priority
BEGIN
IF repair.LifeThreatening THEN priority : = 1
ELSE
IF repair.PropertyThreatening THEN priority : = 2
ELSE
IF (tenant.disabled) OR
(tenant.elderly)   OR
(babies > 0) THEN priority : = 3
ELSE
IF (repair.MinorRepair) THEN priority : = 4
ELSE priority : = 5 ;
END ;
```

Tab. 10.7 Object-oriented PASCAL code (cont'd).

ncreasing popularity of C, means that in its object-oriented form as C + +, the possibilities for expert databases based upon frame-based reasoning and data represented within objects are increasing.

The final implementation path available makes use of some of the modern PROLOG environments which incorporate an integrated database management system. These were initially made available for PCs, but have now been made available for environments suited to larger applications.

Within these environments, the interface is provided for you by the PROLOG environment. However, the interface provided will vary from application to application, and so it is worth investigating whether a particular environment provides the required facilities both for the database and its interface to the expert system component. Some of the recent expert system shells also have integrated DBMS facilities or extensive interfacing facilities. These should also be investigated to see whether the facilities provided are adequate.

The three methods of implementation available within the data-centred approach are compared in Tab. 10.8.

	Advantages	Disadvantages
PROLOG + 4GL + Interface	Flexibility 4GL ideal for DBMS Allows use of tools	Complexity Integrity Maintenance
Object Oriented Language	Integration	Lack of acceptance of OOPS techniques Limitations of frames for knowledge representation
Integrated PROLOG/ DBMS	Convenience	Constraints upon interface and/or DBMS and/or PROLOG implementation

Tab. 10.8 Media for the data-centred approach.

10.4 Strategy 3: The prototyping and porting (ProP) approach

This strategy is for those people who want a expert system but are told that they must produce an information system, to conform to external expectations or standards. This approach has a number of deliverables in a sequential development process. The first deliverable is a prototype system.

The prototype system must handle all the functionality of the problem, but does not have to conform to the full specification in terms of speed performance and method of implementation. It should be developed in such a way as to allow investigation of how it performs, typically within an AI toolkit environment, upon a powerful graphics workstation.

The intermediate system is a complete rewrite of the prototype. It builds upon the experience gained in developing the prototype. It should be developed in a transparent well-structured language, generally C or Pascal. Where this version conforms to expectations or standards, it becomes the final version.

In other cases, the final system is developed using the data structures and design of the intermediate version. The implementation is carried out in the language required by external standards or expectations. This approach is summarized in Fig. 10.13.

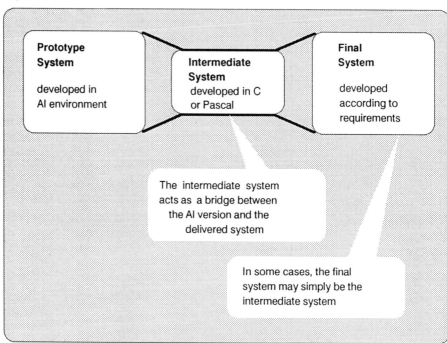

Fig. 10.13 The PROtotyping and Porting approach.

This approach is based upon the work of Dunkelberger (1989) described in Chapter 8. Each stage will be considered in greater detail.

10.4.1 Development of the prototype system

The aim of prototype development is to prove that a system is feasible. Once this is proved, the prototype may then be used to investigate how an intermediate system could be implemented.

The development of the prototype follows traditional expert system development lines. The knowledge must be gathered from available sources. Dunkelberger (*ibid*) employed book knowledge and knowledge elicited from human experts. The elicited knowledge must be represented using one of the available knowledge representation schemes. A typical AI toolkit is invaluable here providing a range of knowledge representation schemes to suit a variety of problems. It is worth remembering, though, that at some point the prototype must be translated into a more constrained environment. In particular, it is important to monitor the prototype to prevent a combinatorial explosion, leading to a system which can never be practically implemented.

The AI toolkit is also helpful in allowing the prototype to be thoroughly investigated tested and modified in a RUDE-based cycle. The end result should be a system that works, together with an understanding of how it works and where its weaknesses lie, especially in terms of performance.

Alongside the prototype system, consideration should be given to an appropriate user interface. The starting point for this is a user model. The prototype interface may be developed on paper, or using a computer drawing package or better still, an interface prototyping tool.

10.4.2 Development of the intermediate system

In developing the intermediate system, three objectives are set out:

- translation into a structured format,
- improvement in performance,
- integration of system and interface.

For the development of the intermediate system, the use of C or Pascal is recommended, because of their transparency and innate structuredness. The system may no longer be constructed in the specialist AI data structures of the prototype. Using the prototype as a guide, the designer is advised to structure the problem, and then examine how each part of the problem has been handled in the prototype solution. Some parts of the problem may well lend themselves to algorithmic solutions, and these may be implemented with a resulting improvement in performance. Many of the AI representations can be directly represented in terms of constructs with C or PASCAL e.g. rules may be represented in terms of simple propositional logic. The use of special features such as object-oriented extensions should be avoided unless they are allowed in the final destination system. It is possible to simulate many features of object-oriented programs using standard code.

Although this approach is primarily sequential, a degree of iteration is acceptable between the prototype development and the intermediate system design. The job of the prototype is to structure the problem sufficiently for the intermediate system designer to develop a structured system. If this proves too difficult, then it is better to return to investigate the prototype further than to persist with a design process going nowhere.

This approach is in some ways the most dependent upon the creativity of the system developer, particularly in translating the AI prototype system into a working structured intermediate. However, the use of tools, a good AI toolkit for prototype development and a front end CASE tool for the structured analysis will certainly help. In a team project, the intermediate system developer should take part in the knowledge elicitation procedure, since the greatest asset of all is a thorough knowledge of the problem, and a richer understanding is gained from the knowledge elicitation process than from the final elicited knowledge.

This intermediate version should be subjected to both unit and system testing, since errors should be eliminated at this stage, before final development.

10.4.3 The final delivered system

The final system in some cases may be the intermediate version. However, in many cases, such as that described by Dunkelberger, the intermediate is used to define the data and coding structures from which the final system is produced.

The step from intermediate to final system should be considerably smaller than from prototype to intermediate. The design work is done, the job is simply to recode the data structures and procedures from the structured intermediate into the final form demanded by the customer.

The final system should be tested to ensure that errors have not been introduced in the recoding process. The system should also be subjected to acceptance testing to ensure that the system meets the customer requirements.

The problems with this approach are the cost of developing three separate systems, and the potential headaches in translating prototype system into a structured intermediate. This problem will increase with the complexity of the system, and it may be that complex applications may have to be tackled as a series of smaller problems. This may not always be possible.

10.5 Other strategies

A number of strategies have been suggested. The list is not exhaustive or complete. The justification for the strategies contained in this chapter has been simply that they worked for someone somewhere with a particular problem.

Faced with a problem, the system designer is recommended to adopt the following approach:

First, try an existing strategy. Three strategies have been suggested here which between them cover a range of problems. The strategies are not cast in stone. An attempt has been made to show how they may be varied to suit local conditions, and individual preferences. For example, in Dunkelberger's original work, he used C for his intermediate system and successfully translated it into the final Ada system. The author prefers to use PASCAL because of its greater transparency.

Secondly, try to adapt it. System development methodologies are generally intended to be followed rigidly, particularly those based upon the sequential waterfall lifecycle model. In practice, they are often applied in a more flexible manner. The ill-defined nature of expert system problems does not lend itself to the rigid application of a methodology. Therefore, if the strategies presented are unsuitable, it is worth examining why they are unsuitable and trying to address the limitation by adaptation. In practice, most 'new' methodologies are arrived at in this way, being an adaptation and combination of existing development strategies.

Thirdly, develop your own from scratch. This option is not as desperate as it sounds, or as attractive. The biggest mistake that can be made is to ignore the wealth of previous experience in system development, to spend much effort re-inventing the wheel. Some of the workers in the AI field appear to have wilfully ignored the lessons learnt in software engineering in the past, e.g. the experience with evolutionary system development (Gilb,1988). Anyone who wishes to start from scratch requires a thorough knowledge of what has been done in software engineering, expert systems and integration of the two disciplines. Hopefully, this book has provided some of the required information.

The final comment on development strategies must be that a development strategy stands and falls by the quality of the resulting solutions, and the effort required to produce them, and not by any intrinsic merit.

10.6 Further reading

The strategies discussed in this chapter are based upon the ideas presented in the rest of the work. If you have read this chapter first, go back and read the rest of the book!

CHAPTER ELEVEN

Conclusions

The concluding chapter is a summary of the current and future importance of the integration of expert systems into mainstream software. The author believes there have been positive developments accompanied by a change in attitude even whilst the book has been written. The future for integrated expert systems looks both encouraging and challenging.

11.1 The current situation

When this book was first conceived in 1988, the idea of integrating expert systems was still a very novel one for many people. In the academic community in particular, there was a sense in which this was seen as defeatist and demeaning to AI. There are still those who feel this way. However, perhaps because the popularity of expert systems as an AI technique appears to have waned somewhat, expert systems have been left in the hands of people more concerned with solving problems. Amongst such practitioners, the idea of integration is likely to be more acceptable. This may, in fact, lead to further separation of 'expert systems' from the academic AI community, as expert systems become more involved with other software disciplines.

A number of pieces of evidence have emerged to support the theory that integration is becoming more acceptable, and is often considered desirable.

- Integrated tools are emerging to support integrated system implementation. Examples include PROLOG environments with integrated databases, PROLOG compilers with the ability to call and be called from other languages such as C, expert system shells with integrated databases, and fourth generation languages with the facilities to handle objects and rules.
- A number of books are emerging promoting the virtues of integrated expert database systems e.g. Beynon-Davis (1990).
- At a recent AI conference in the USA, one of the pioneers in the AI field, involved in the development of the MYCIN and PROSPECTOR expert systems, gave an invited lecture entitled 'Styles of programming in expert systems and neural networks' emphasizing that these AI technologies were simply another style of computer programming. (Duda, 1989).

There is a danger, however, associated with such a trend. The uptake of many information-based technologies appears to form an almost Normal distribution over time (Fig 11.1).

Popularity

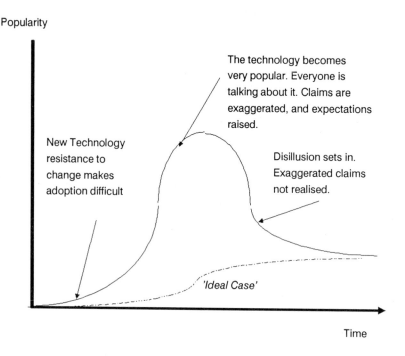

The technology becomes very popular. Everyone is talking about it. Claims are exaggerated, and expectations raised.

New Technology resistance to change makes adoption difficult

Disillusion sets in. Exaggerated claims not realised.

'Ideal Case'

Time

Fig. 11.1 Information technology lifecycle.

Initially, the new technique or technology struggles against people's natural resistance to change. If it overcomes this problem, it then becomes the latest new technology. It is adopted with great gusto by many people. They get carried away and present it as a universal panacea. Unrealistic claims are made. If the claims are genuinely unrealistic, then disillusionment sets in and people start to point out the limitations of the technique. The popularity falls away and many people move on to the next technology that comes along. What is left is a small group of people with a realistic appreciation of the strengths and weaknesses who as a consequence are able to apply it in a meaningful way to solve problems.

Expert systems may be seen as one technology which has followed this pattern: a period of hype, followed by a period of disillusionment. CASE tools are currently enjoying a period of great popularity, but a number of authors are already suggesting that this honeymoon period is drawing to a close. The ideal transition is to reach the steady-state case without having to go through these periods of expectation and disillusionment. This is more likely to happen when the technology concerned is forced to justify itself on its own merits. Thus, the aim of this book has been to show where integration may be used effectively, rather than to promote the use of integrated expert systems for their own sake. The measure of its success will be the acceptance of the underlying principle of integration - the targeting of the most appropriate technology to the correct parts of the problem, rather than a rash of integrated systems introduced because the idea has suddenly become fashionable.

11.2 The future

The future for integration looks bright. We may consider this by returning to the three level model which we started with in Chapter 1.

11.2.1 The future of integration at the concept level

The introduction of ideas from expert systems into mainstream software and vice versa can only be beneficial. Dissatisfaction with the rigid sequential waterfall model of software development has been expressed by many, particularly in the area of meeting user needs. Software engineering can benefit here from expert system ideas of knowledge elicitation, and also the use of evolutionary development techniques. The realization amongst expert systems developers that the uses of such systems may be substantially wider than the traditional role of consultation suggests that techniques of user modelling can be employed to boost the usefulness of expert systems.

The introduction of standards to promote software quality is likely to force expert system designers to adopt software engineering practices and methodologies. The work of Dunkelberger suggests that this may be viewed as a challenge rather than a handicap. Whilst standards cannot provide the whole solution to the quality issues, they should prevent the worst systems from seeing the light of day, and ensuring a certain minimum standard of technical quality.

11.2.2 The future of integration at the data level

The expert database system has emerged as a distinct type of system in its own right. Suppliers of tools to assist in the development of both DBMS and expert systems have recognized the need for providing facilities for integration: database management facilities within expert system shells and PROLOG environments, and data structures to handle rules and objects in third- and fourth-generation languages.

There are specific problems emerging from the use of DBMSs, which integrating expert systems can address. Many database users complain of an 'information overload' problem. Expert systems can reduce the amount of information that the user has to interpret, and ensure that the information produced is appropriate to the user's requirements.

The most elegant type of solution for an integrated expert database system remains a system based upon logic and implemented in PROLOG. The practical problems associated with a large database implemented in this way suggest that we shall remain with coupled systems for some time to come.

11.2.3 The future of integration at the coding level

Systems integrated at the coding level are dependent upon the provision of the correct tools and languages for the system developer. However, this has been used in the past to justify the exclusivity of 'stand-alone' systems. Knowledge-based systems have been written in such simple languages as BASIC. Of course, fully-fledged expert systems with their associated complexity are not generally written in BASIC, but neither are complex information systems. The future is likely to be easier for integrated system developers as suitable tools are designed and made available. The advent of object-oriented dialects of C and Pascal is one example which is already available.

11.3 The final word

The sole reason for adopting an integrated approach is to provide better solutions. If this is achieved, then the integrated approach will be embraced enthusiastically. If this is not achieved, then it has no reason left to exist.

References

Alexsander, I. (ed) (1989) *Neural Computing Architectures*, North Oxford Academic: London.

Ashworth, C and Goodland, M. (1990), *SSADM: A practical approach*, Graw-Hill.

Basden, A. (1983) On the application of expert systems, *Int. J. Man-Machine Studies*,(19), 461–77.

Berry, D. C. and Broadbent, D. E. (1986, 1987) Expert systems and the man-machine interface, Exp. Sys. 3(4) and 4(1).

Berry, D. C. and Hart, A. (eds)(1989) *Expert Systems: Human Issues, Kogan Page, London.*

Beynon–Davis, P. (1991) *Expert database systems*, Graw–Hill.

Boehm, B. *et al.* , (1978) *Characteristics of software quality*, North-Holland, New York.

Boehm, B. (1981) *Software Engineering Economics*, Prentice-Hall.

Buchanan, B. G. (1986) Expert Systems: working systems and the research literature, *Exp. Systems*, 3(1).

Chen, E. T. (1978) Program complexity and programmer productivity, *IEEE Trans. Soft. Eng., SE-4*, (3) 187–94.

Clocksin, W. F. and Mellish, C.S. (1987) *Programming in PROLOG*, (3rd edn.), Springer–Verlag, N.Y.

Coats, R. B. and Vlaeminke, I. (1987) *Man-Computer interfaces: An introduction to Software Design and Implementation*, Blackwell, Oxford.

Collins, H. M. (1987) *Expert systems, artificial intelligence and the behavioural co-ordinates of skill*, in B. Bloomfield (ed). *The question of Artificial Intelligence: Philosophical and Sociological Perspectives*, Croom-Helm.

Davis, J. S. (1984)Chunks: a basis for complexity measurement, *Information Processing and Management Theoretical Computing Science*, (38) 145-71.

DeMarco, T. (1979)*Structured Analysis and System Specification*, Englewood Cliffs, Yourdon Press.

DeYoung, G. E. and Kampe, G. R. (1979) Program factors as predictors of program reliability, *Proc comp. software and applications software conf, IEEE,* 668–73.

Dreyfus, S. E. (1985) The nature of Expertise, *IJCAI 85,* **2** 1306.

Duda, R. O. (1989) Styles of programming in neural networks and expert systems, *Proc. Applications of AI* **VII** *conference, Orlando,* SPIE (1095) 559–68.

Duda, R. O. and Reboh, R. (1984) AI and decision making: the PROSPECTOR experience in *Artificial Intelligence in Business, (ed. W. Reitmann), Ablex, N. J.,* 111–47.

Duda, R. O and Shortliffe, E. H. (1983) Expert systems research, *Science,* **220,** 261–8.

Dunkelberger, K. A. (1989) OFC: a deliverable military planning aid, *Proc. Applications of AI* **VII** *conference, Orlando,* SPIE (1095) 725–34.

Feuer, A. R. and Fowlkes, E. B. (1979) Relating computer program reliability to software measures, *Proc. Nat. Comp. Conf.,* IEEE, 1003–12.

Feuer, A. R. and Fowlkes, E. B. (1979) Some results from an empirical study of computer software, *Proc. 4th Int. Conf. on Soft. Eng.,* IEEE, 351–5.

Fisher, A. S. (1988) *CASE: Tools for software development,* Wiley, New York.

Funami, Y. and Halstead, M. H. (1975) *A software physics analysis of Akiyama's debugging data,* Lafayette.

Gachnig, J. Klahr, P. Pople, H. Shortliffe, E. and Terry, A. (1983) Evaluation of expert systems: issues and case studies in *Building Expert Systems* (eds. Hayes-Roth, F. Waterman, D. and Lenat, D. B.).

Garvin, D. (1984) What does product quality mean? *Sloan Management Review,* (4).

Gilb, T. (1977) *Software Metrics,* Winthrop.

Gilb, T. (1988) *Principles of Software Engineering Management,* Addison-Wesley.

Gillies, A. C. (1990a) Towards a user oriented model of software quality (1): A knowledge elicitation exercise, (submitted to) *Software: Practice and Experience.*

Gillies, A. C. (1990b) Towards a user oriented model of software quality (2): A new hierarchical model of quality, (submitted to) *Software: Practice and Experience.*

Gillies, A. C. and Hart, A. E. (1989a) Using knowledge-based ideas in image processing: A case study in human computer interaction, *Proc. BCS Expert Systems Conf ES88,* Brighton, UK, CUP.

Gillies, A. C. and Hart, A. E. (1989b) Using Knowledge to enhance the scope and efficiency of image processing in fringe analysis, *Proc. Applications of AI* **VII** *conference, Orlando, SPIE (1095) 742–50.*

Gillies, A. C. and Hart, A. E. (1991) On the Use of Graphical Techniques to Display Profiles and Quality, (submitted to) *Total Quality Management.*

Gillies, A. C, Keskin, O. Telfer, D. J. and Whiteley, K. (1988) The use of a priori knowledge in the analysis of fringe patterns, *Proc. Int. Conf. Opt. Eng, Industrial Inspection, Hamburg,* SPIE (1010), 44-50.

Gong, H. and Schmidt, M. (1988). A complexity measure based upon selection and nesting, *ACM Sigmetrics.*

Gordon, R. D. (1979) Measuring improvements in program clarity, *IEEE Trans. Soft. Eng.,* **SE-5**, (2) , 79-90.

Gunning, R. (1968) *The technique of clear writing,* Graw-Hill.

Halstead, M. H. (1977) *Elements of Software Science,* Elsevier.

Hansen, W. J. (1978) Measurement of program complexity by the pair (cyclomatic number, output count) *ACM SIGPLAN notices,* (4), 29–33.

Hart, A. (1987) Role of induction in knowledge elicitation in *Knowledge Acquisition: a practical Casebook* (ed. A. Kidd), Plenum Press.

Hart, A. (1989) *Knowledge Acquistion For Expert Systems,* 2nd Edn., Chapman-Hall, London.

Hendry, A. W. (1966)*Photoelastic Stress Analysis,* Pergammon.

Henry. S. and Kafura, D. (1981) Software structure metrics based upon information flow, *IEEE Trans. Soft. Eng,* **SE-7**, (5) 510–8.

Ince D. C. (1988) System Complexity, *Information Technology Briefings,* Open University.

Jacob, R. J. K. (1985) Designing expert systems for ease of change, *Proc IEEE Symposium on Expert systems in Government,* 246–51.

Jarke, M. J and Vassiliou, (1984) Coupling expert systems with database management systems, *Artificial Intelligence for Business,* Ablex.

Jorgensen, A. H. (1980) A methodology for measuring the readability and modifiability of programs, *BIT,* (20) 394–405.

Kafura, D. and Henry, S. (1981) Software quality metrics based upon interconnectivity, *Journal of Systems and Software,* (2), 121–31.

Kepner, C. H. and Tregoe, B. B. (1981) Entscheidungen vorbereiten und richtig treffen. Rationales Management:die neue Herausforderung, *Verlag Moderne Industrie*. (in German). Work cited in English in Watts (1987) *Measuring Software Quality*, NCC Publications.

Kincaid, J. P. *et al* (1981), Computer readability editing system, *IEEE Trans Prof. Comm.* , **PC-24**, (1) 38–41.

Kitchenham, B. (1989) Software quality assurance   *Microprocessors and Microcomputers*, **13**, (6) 373–81.

Kitchenham, B. (1989) Software Metrics in (ed. Rook, P.) *Software Reliability Handbook*, Elsevier.

Land, L. and Mulhall, T.   (1989) Developing co-operative knowledge-based systems, *Proc. BCS Expert Systems Conf ES89*, London, UK, CUP, 90–103.

Liebowitz, J. (1986) Useful approach for evaluating expert systems, *Expert Systems*, **3** (2) 86-96.

Lindsay, R., Buchanan, B. G., Feigenbaum, E. A. and Lederburg, J. (1980) *DENDRAL*, McGraw-Hill.

Lippman, S. B. *A C + + Primer*, Addison–Wesley.

Long, J. and Dowell, J. (1989) Conceptions of the discipline of HCI: Craft, Applied Science, and Engineering , *Proc. BCS HCISG Conf People and Computers***V**, 9-34, CUP.

Lantz, K. E. (1989) *The Prototyping Methodology*, Prentice-Hall, New Jersey.

Lu, H. E and Wang, P. S. P. (1986) A comment on 'A Fast Parallel Algorithm for Thinning Digital Patterns, *Comm. ACM*, **29** (3), 239–242.

Maier, H. H. (1983) Die Prufung des Software-Qualitatsmerkmals Benutzungsfreundlichkeit, *QZ Management der Qualitatssicherung*, **1** (28) (in German). Work cited in English in Watts, R. (1987) *Measuring Software Quality*, NCC Publications.

Martin J. (1988) *An Introduction To Information Engineering*, Texas Instruments.

McCabe, T. J. (1976) A Complexity measure, *IEEE Trans. Soft. Eng.*, **SE-2**, *(4) 308-20.*

McCall, J. A. (1980). An assessment of current software metric research, *Proceedings EASCON80*, IEEE, 323-33.

McCall, J. A et al (1977) Concepts and definitions of software quality, *Factors in software quality*, NTIS, **1**.

McClure, C. L. (1978) A model for program complexity analysis, *Proc 3rd Int Conf. Soft. Eng.* , IEEE, 149-57.

McDermott, J. (1985) Doing R1 with style, *2nd conf on AI appl.*, Miami.

Michie, D. and Johnson, R. (1985) *The Creative Computer*, Pelican, London.

Modesitt, K. L. (1987) Experts: Human and otherwise, *Proc. 3rd Int. Exp. Systems Conf.*, Learned Information, Oxford, 333-42.

Mohanty, S. N. and Adamowicz, M. (1976) Proposed measures for the evaluation of software *Proc. Symposium on Computer Soft. Eng.*, MRI, New York Polytechnic, 485-97.

Musa, J. D. (1975) A theory of software reliability and its applications *IEEE Trans. Soft. Eng.*, **SE-1**, 312-7.

Myers, G. J. (1976) *Software reliability: principles and practice*, Wiley.

NIP Prolog (1985), Edinburgh University.

O'Neill, M. and Morris, A. (1989) Expert Systems in the United Kingdom: an evaluation of development methodologies *Exp. Sys.*, **6** (2) 90-9.

Ostberg, O. (1988) Applying expert systems technology, in *Knowledge, Skill, and Artificial Intelligence* (eds. Goranzon, B. and Josefson, I.), Springer–Verlag, Cambridge.

Ottenstein, L. M. (1981) Predicting numbers of errors using software science *Proc. ACM annual conference*, ACM, 157-67.

Oviedo, E. I. (1980) Control flow, data flow and program complexity, *Proc of the computer software and applications conf.*, IEEE.

Paige, M. (1980) A metric for software test planning, *Proc of the computer software and applications conf.*, IEEE, 499-504.

Parnas, D. L. (1979) Designing Software for ease of extension and contraction, *IEEE Trans. Soft. Eng.*, **SE-5**, 128 *et seq.*

Partridge, D. (1986) *Artificial Intelligence: applications in the future of software engineering*, Ellis-Horwood, Chichester.

Perry, W. (1983) *Effective Methods of EDP Quality Assurance*, Prentice-Hall.

Pew, R. W. (1983) Human Skills and their utilisation, *Man/machine Interface Symposium*, CEI Europe, June, cited in Salmon, R. and Slater, M. (1987)*Computer Graphics: Systems and Concepts*, Addison–Wesley.

Remus H. and Zilles, S. (1981) Prediction and management of program quality, *Proc 4th Int. Conf. on Soft. Eng.*, IEEE, 341-50.

Rumelhart, D. E and McClelland, J. L (1986) *Parallel Distributed Processing* 1 and 2, MIT Press: Cambridge, Mass.

Scheifler, R. W. et al (1986) The X Window System, Trans. Graph #63, Special Issue on User Interface Software, ACM.

Schmitz, P. et al, (1975) Ein Kombinationsverfahren fur Rangfolgeentscheidungen Schriftreihe des Rechenzentrums der Universitaat zu Koln, 23.(in German). Work cited in English in Watts, R. (1987) *Measuring Software Quality*, NCC Publications.

Shammas, N. (1989) *Object-oriented programming with Turbo Pascal*, Wiley, New York.

Shortliffe, E. H. (1976)*Computer-Based Medical Consultations: MYCIN*, American Elsevier.

Sommerville, I. (1989) *Software Engineering*, 3rd edn, Addison-Wesley.

Southwick, R. W. (1989) Topic explanation in expert systems, *Proc. BCS Expert Systems Conf ES89*, London, UK, CUP, 47–57.

Sleeman, D. and Ward, R. D. (1989) Intelligent tutoring systems in training and education: Prospects and Problems, *Proc. BCS Expert Systems Conf ES89*, London, UK, CUP, 331–43.

Stonebraker, M. E. , Wong, E, and Krep, P. , (1986) The design and implementation of Ingres, *ACM Trans. Database Systems*, 1, (3) 189-222.

Swartout, W. R. (1983) XPLAIN: a system for creating and explaining expert consulting programs, *Art. Intell.*, 21, 285–325.

Tang, H. , Major, N. and Rivers, R. (1989) 'From Users to Dialogues: Enabling authors to Build an Adaptive , Intelligent System, *Proc. BCS HCISG Conf People and Computers* V, **CUP, 121-36.**

Thayer, T. A. et al (1977) Software reliability study, *TRW-SS-76-03*, IEEE Computing Society.

Torsun, I. S. (1987) PAYE: A tax expert system, *Proc. BCS Expert Systems Conf ES86*, Brighton, CUP, 69–80.

Torsun, I. S. and Ng, Y. M. TCEDI: An expert database system interface, *Proc. BCS Expert Systems Conf ES86*, Brighton, CUP, 210–23.

Walters, J. R. and Nielsen, N. R (1988) *Crafting Knowledge-Based Systems*, Wiley, New York.

Waterman, D. (1986) *A Guide To Expert Systems,* Addison-Wesley

Watts, R. (1987) *Measuring Software Quality*, NCC Publications.

Woodward, M. R. *et al* (1980) Experience with path analysis and testing programs *IEEE Trans Soft. Eng.*, **SE-6**, (6) 278–86.

Yasuda, K. (1989) Software Quality Assurance Activities In Japan in *Japanese Perspectives In Software Engineering*, Addison-Wesley.

Yau, S. S. and Collofello, J. S. (1979) Some stability measures for software maintenance *Proc. of the computer software and applications conf.*, IEEE.

Yin, B. H. (1979) Software design testability analysis *Proc of the computer software and applications conf.*, IEEE, 729–34.

Yin, B. H. and Winchester, J. W. (1978) The establishment and use of measures to evaluate the quality of software designs, *ACM Software Engineering Notes*, **3**, (5) 45–52.

Zhang, T. Y. and Suen, C. Y. (1984) A Fast Parallel Algorithm for Thinning Digital Patterns, *Comm. ACM.*, **27** (3) 236-39.

Zolnowski, J. M. and Simmons, D. B. (1979) A complexity measure applied to Fortran *Proc of the computer software and applications conf.*, IEEE.

Index